AF250299

# THE EMOTIONALLY UNAVAILABLE MAN
## Can he fall in love with you?

# THE EMOTIONALLY UNAVAILABLE MAN

## Can he fall in love with you?

---

By

Lilith White

ISBN  978-0-6398311-0-7

Enquiries welcome: authorlilithwhite@gmail.com

Your love is not dependent
On outer circumstances
Or whether or not it is returned to you
There is a freedom in knowing
That you are free to love
Whoever you choose
You don't have to stop the flow of love
Just the expectation and longing
That love has created in you
Let go of the story
And live your authentic life in love.

**Lilith White**

# Acknowledgements

The writing of a book is done in isolation and a non-fiction is always just a snippet of the author's life experience - a central theme like a play being played out on a stage. There are so many other things happening in the wings that are not mentioned. This is where the author gets the opportunity to pay homage to the people who have contributed to their journey and have helped, either physically or supportively to the coming into being of their published book.

Enes - For being the emotionally unavailable man in this book - you came into my life to teach me more about myself. It was through you that I gained the insights into the content of this book. You have indirectly helped the many women who will read and learn from my experience. Through this process I was better able to understand this dimension of the male psyche and relationships. I will always admire the amazing man that you are.

Annie – A big thank you for my beautiful, bright cover design and for the rope around the heart illustration. You are a true artist. You also went above and beyond to help me with the proof reading of this book. Through all the years I have known you, you have supported me through various phases of my life and I am eternally grateful to you for your ongoing love and friendship.

My daughter - You are the rainbow in my life. No matter what I share with you, you always remind me of the powerful, wild woman that I, intrinsically, am. Not only have you physically supported my writing by reading and commenting on the manuscript of this book but you have also always been there when I needed to be vulnerable. Thank you my angel for your unconditional love and for believing in me.

My son - You were my rock during my hospitalisation and my support system in my recovery.  You are an amazing human being - always solid and a grounding force in my life.

Deborah at Skoobs Theatre of Books - Thank you for being my muse. Your love of my writing has inspired me to believe more fully in my gift.

Clinton  -  Without you, I would have fallen into oblivion many times in my life. Thank you for all the times you held my hand and for your eternal love and unconditional friendship.

# Content


Prologue

Meeting My Emotionally Unavailable Mr. Right… 1

The Journal and Insights… 7

<u>What You Can and Can't Expect From</u>
<u>An Emotionally Unavailable Man:</u>
How to Survive an Emotionally Unavailable Man… 110
The Woman Who Fall for Emotionally Unavailable Men… 111
How do I Deserve to be Treated?... 112
Sex and the Emotionally Unavailable Man… 113
Can an Emotionally Unavailable Man be a Nice Guy?... 115
Can You Just be His Friend?... 115
Positive Steps to Recreate Your Social Life… 116
Can an Emotionally Unavailable Man Fall in Love with You?... 117

Afterword: Two Years Later…121
Poem for Enes – Simpatico…122

# Prologue

The day I met Enes, he told me he was *happily single*. I smiled and told him, so was I. I never imagined that happily single meant *unavailable*. There are millions of people, across the globe, pretty content with their single lives, but when someone comes around, knocks their socks off, spins them around and sweeps them off their feet, they become happily *un-single*. It took me a while to figure out that he really and truly was *emotionally unavailable*, and what that meant to our future relationship prospects or should I rather say... lack of them.

If you have never before been in the unfortunate situation of falling for an emotionally unavailable man, like me, you will have no way of knowing that this man has made a conscious decision, at some point, that relationships are just not for them and they mean it. Some of them admit it to themselves, others don't. Some of them will happily have, no strings attached sex, others won't. All of them have their own stories. Whether it stemmed from their childhood or whether it stemmed from traumatic relationships in their past or whatever their unique reason is, they are highly unlikely to share any of it with you. They may be upfront with you about where you stand or they may not be, so it could take you a while to figure out - even though this man is paying you a lot of attention, he is not going to be your boyfriend.

He may behave a bit like that guy, you have always dreamed about, arriving on his stallion to sweep you up and carry you to his cave but more often than not, you'll be left wondering where you stand with him and you are likely to end up asking yourself if he is really worth your time and effort.

In my case, things looked very positive for a potential relationship. Because we had both been single for a long time, I assumed that we were equally happy to *take it slow*. I respected him for not diving in head first and for not trying to take advantage of me sexually. I was perfectly content to allow it to grow in its own time but then realised it was progressing a little bit too slowly. I began feeling frustrated with the *not knowing where I stood* or where it was potentially going – utterly confused actually.

The beginning stages, of most relationships, come with their own set of challenges. Both parties are usually dealing with a certain amount of new relationship anxiety. I thought it was healthy that we were keeping an emotional distance during the *checking it out* stage. It made a lot of sense. I convinced myself that after so many whirlwind type beginnings, in my past, we were building a strong foundation for the future. Eventually I began to realise that if this new relationship could be likened to a plane on a runway - it was never going to leave the airport and it was failing completely, to launch. Something just didn't feel right. If anything, the pilot steering this plane, seemed intoxicated and was simply going around in circles.

The only way, I can describe this is that it just wasn't *flowing* like the normal dating stage of a new relationship. Usually, after a successful date, phone calls are made or text messages are sent, to arrange the next meeting. We had such a good time together - surely he would want to see me again as much as I wanted to see him? He had even messaged me to thank me and tell me what a lovely time he had. He seemed just as interested as I was. With an emotionally unavailable man, it becomes a guessing game.

Enes behaved really interested at times. There were even outreaches that could have been misconstrued as romantic, but then I would be left hanging. He didn't behave like he was not interested but his advances were puzzling - they never progressed into a more tangible, desire for *real sharing*. I am sure there are a myriad of variations to this scenario but at the end of the day, women who are dating emotionally unavailable men, are generally left feeling utterly bewildered. Are you a part of his life or not? Is he ever going to include you in his social circle? Are you going to start spending more quality time together? Is the relationship going to grow and evolve? Why is he being so avoidant?

In the beginning it was exciting as I began realising that I was falling hard for this man and was convinced that he felt the same. At times, I believed he would definitely end up being my boyfriend. It was just a matter of time. He was kind, considerate, and our almost daily text messages evolved into emails, where we began sharing more openly and deeply about life. He seemed to *get me* and was always willing to share advice and give verbal support. I did notice that he didn't share too much about himself on a personal level, which niggled at me a bit but he was a man after all, and on some level, was actually sharing more than most men. We seemed to be incredibly compatible. I believed a miracle had arrived in my life. I was ecstatic.

When I noticed that he wasn't making too much of an effort to make arrangements to see me face to face, I realised that he was becoming more like a long distance pen pal than anything else, but he was very dedicated to his job, to the point of being a workaholic. This in itself didn't put me off. He was successful and because I was used to spending loads of time alone, I didn't see his dedication to his job as a long term issue.

It was only when I started thinking more in depth about it that I realised that we hadn't actually spent much *real* time together. This was when I started wondering if perhaps he had a secret life. He seemed to only want to come to my house for dinner during the week, when he couldn't stay very late. When this didn't develop into spending time on weekends, I started getting suspicious. Maybe he was actually gay or had another woman on the go. I didn't feel entitled to question him about his life. We weren't even in a physical relationship, so I felt a bit ridiculous thinking of him as anything more than a friend. But we were having daily contact, which wasn't usual for a new, *just a friend.*

I found myself getting lost, in a quagmire of thoughts of longing and desire for him as I began losing my balance in self doubt. The first stages of falling in love are sometimes referred to as a type of madness or mania and I would spend days, engrossed in my journal or self-absorption, with little to no social life or outside contact. Before I knew it, I found myself immersed in despair. Unrequited love has been written about by poets and writers throughout the ages. I never intended to publish my journal but I have since researched and explored the emotionally unavailable man and his avoidant style of relating and realised that by sharing my memoir, I can help other women better understand why falling for and surviving an emotionally unavailable man can be so painful and soul destroying.

Interwoven, in my own personal story, I have included many of the insights I have since gained and helpful suggestions about how to better deal with the feelings of uncertainty and rejection that you may be experiencing.

It's up to each woman, as an individual, to decide what they will or won't put up with. The best way to reach this decision is to arm yourself with knowledge to enable you to make an informed choice. I hope that my experience will help you to do this. If you are questioning whether or not you have fallen for an emotionally unavailable man, I suspect, the mere fact that you were attracted to and opened this book, means that you have. If so, by the end of this book, you will know for sure. My story will give you all the clues to look out for. The last chapter of the book is dedicated to pointers and information that you will find very helpful and enlightening.

Can an emotionally unavailable man fall in love with you? Yes, of course he can – nobody is immune to love but he may never act on it or may never admit it, either to you or himself. Fasten you safety belt while I take you along with me on my journey through my emotionally unavailable amusement park, filled with stomach churning Ferris Wheels, sometimes the dumping and diving of the big dipper, but mostly to the ceaseless, giddiness of merry-go-rounds.

# Meeting My Emotionally Unavailable Mr. Right



It was two months, almost to the day, that I had gone into hospital with blood in my urine and severe stomach cramps and had landed up in ICU, fighting for my life, with Pancreatitis. I had come out of hospital too weak to make food or even wash dishes and had lost a valuable organ, my gall bladder. I was clearly on the road to recovery but was still finding my feet. My diet had changed drastically and I had to relearn what I could and couldn't eat. It was a process.

The last thing I felt like doing was going out to a social event. The furthest I had driven was to the shops and this *get together* required traipsing all the way across town. Under normal circumstances, before my medical emergency, I was already socially challenged. It would take a lot for me to go out anywhere. This seemed like a mammoth task. My friend, Kendall, was leaving to work in the UK and was having a farewell. She had begged me to come. To be honest, it sounded more like she needed numbers when she told me that so few people had actually sent her an RSVP. Besides that, she never visited me in hospital nor had she made any effort since. I really didn't feel like I owed her anything but I decided to see it differently. It was an opportunity to get out of the house. At some point, I had to face taking baby steps back into the world and this was an opportunity to do just that. I decided to go. I could leave when I wanted. What did I have to lose?

The last thing I had on my mind, was meeting a man. I was feeling vulnerable just facing the drive and a crowd of people - and I had to do it sober, without any mind relaxing social crutches. I wasn't really drinking much before the Pancreatitis but I was not allowed a drop for six months and I, quite honestly, had absolutely no desire to drink. Just being there would be a marvel, without any other agendas. Getting there, spending a bit of time and leaving would be enough of a giant leap for me. Those simple actions, we generally take for granted, would be empowering.

I have known many of Kendall's friends for years but have always felt on the outskirts of the crowd, like I belonged to the tribe yet I had never quite belonged. I guess I never really felt like I belonged to any group, not really. So I was most surprised by the warm welcome I received. Everybody was overjoyed to see me. It struck me that perhaps they felt closer to me than I had felt to them.

My old friend Dona arrived. She had been another one who knew I was in hospital, but had not visited or even messaged me or my kids to find out how I was doing. I had decided that if I dissociated from everybody who hadn't shown an ounce of concern for me in my darkest hour, I would have no friends. Perhaps they all just had busy lives and their own challenges.

I had also not been smoking cigarettes since ICU. You can't exactly smoke in ICU tied up to machines. Besides, I was too out of it for the first few days on Morphine and pretty much fighting for my life, to even think about smoking. As I started improving though, I realised that if I was going to give up, this would be my opportunity. When I was moved to the general ward, I started craving cigarettes and asked my son to buy me a Vape Pen, which has now become my new *dummy*. I decided to be rebellious and smoke a couple of Dona's cigarettes. We were sitting outside on the lawn when a guy sat down next to me and started chatting to a woman next to him, who he clearly knew. He was tall with an olive complexion, unusual features and a foreign accent and I suddenly remembered that Kendall had mentioned she had a couple of Turkish friends. I had visited Turkey a few years before and when I say that I seldom felt like I belonged, Turkey was, strangely, the one place I had felt a strong sense of *coming home*. It was the last time I could remember feeling completely aligned and good about myself.

"Are you Turkish?" I asked.

He had an incredibly open smile and we immediately got chatting. Yes he was Turkish - his name was Enes. I introduced myself and Dona. I felt immediately animated talking about Turkey and how much I loved his homeland and its people. I told them about staying on a boat for seven days and my dream of going back with a crowd of people because although I loved the experience, I didn't enjoy the spoiled Western youngsters who shared the boat with us. Dona went to mingle, while the Turk and I spoke about a myriad of things, including that we were both *happily single* and I expressed that I would love to meet new people and make new friends. I said I would plan to have a social event in the not too distant future.

When I told him where I lived, he said he had a Turkish friend who lived in the same area. He was an eccentric who was also an engineer but had given it all up to do organic vegetable growing. He said he would come around and pick me up and take me to visit him. I had recently moved to the small country community of Chartwell, on the outskirts of Johannesburg and didn't know anyone in the area. It all sounded quite exciting and meant to be — new future prospects were surprisingly unfolding before my eyes.

I told him about the Pancreatitis. Most people don't have a clue what that even is. I didn't when they came and broke the *'bad news'* to me. He told me he had a friend staying with him after he had come out of hospital with Pancreatitis and he had taken care of him. It was comforting that he knew exactly what I had been through and was still going through.

Enes went off to mingle and at one point I looked up at him — he was standing talking to somebody. As if he had felt my energy he turned around and looked back at me. Although I didn't quite process it immediately, I felt an unusual connection to him and I liked what saw — I hadn't been attracted to a man in years. In retrospect, I think I had already fallen for him. Love, which had come easy to me in my youth, had become an alien concept to me over time. In fact, I had absolutely no concept of what the word even meant. I had given up on finding love a long time ago but in that moment, I knew that he was different and that I already felt a simpatico with him.

A while after eating around a table, sitting close enough to the Turk to be oddly distracted by his alluring vibe, I decided to leave. Dona had left a few minutes before and I was going around saying my goodbyes, when he came and asked me for my phone number – a man I was already attracted to was asking for my phone number.

In the car on the way home, I was finding it difficult to assimilate. I clearly can't remember my exact thoughts but I think this is pretty much how they were running through my mind...*Had I just met a man who was interested in me? We had both said we were happily single but what exactly does that mean? How weird is that – I wasn't going to go. I didn't even spend time with Kendall. She seemed to have had enough people around, not to care about the fact that I had made the effort to come to her farewell. It was almost like the universe had lined me up to go to meet Enes but dare I even think this or project anything on to it? He asked for my phone number. I'd spoken about meeting new friends and future social gatherings - it didn't mean anything – I mustn't place anything on this.* I was already in love with him, even if I, myself, didn't believe it was at all possible.

My excitement wore off when I didn't hear from him, so I tried to put it behind me. He had miss called me straight away so that I could save his number, he said. I knew the best way to see this man again was to organise something at my house but I had a problem knowing who to invite. I actually didn't really want to share him with anybody, so I waited and in the next few weeks, put it to one side. I had my own life to focus on, my own recovery and the most important thing was that I needed to reinvent myself. In places like the US they have Pancreatitis survivor support groups. At this point, I hadn't yet fully integrated the fact that I had nearly died. It didn't even seem real but I would later realise that it had impacted quite profoundly on me.

*When a man tells you he is happily single when he meets you, be warned. He may later turn around and tell you that he was upfront with you from the word go. Happily single may not always translate into emotionally unavailable but listen carefully to what a man tells you. He is telling you something for a reason – perhaps for your own good. If you decide to then go ahead and project a future relationship on to this man and you allow yourself to fall head over heels, you cannot blame him for it later on down the line.*

# The Journal and Insights

## December

### Do I make the first move?

### 19th December - Sunday

I still have a certain amount of confusion about who makes the first move after an exchange of phone numbers. Before cell phones, you would give a guy your number and it would be completely in his hands - you wouldn't even bother to ask him for his. Enes had made a point of *miss calling* me after I gave him my number so the ball was in either one of our courts. We had discussed how nice it would be to meet new friends and I had mentioned that I would have a social event at my place.

I ran it by my son and confidante. He told me it was completely outdated to wait for a man to make the first move. If you like a guy and wanted to connect, it was perfectly cool to contact him. He had made a *point* of *making sure* he had my number before I left, so I decided to make the first move - I took my son's advice and sent Enes a message.

'Hi it's Lesley…I met you at Kendall's farewell. I see you're on whatsapp…hello hehe. Must make a plan for a barbeque or something soonish. Just wanted to connect and say hi.'

'Hello Lesley how nice to hear from you…soon after that night I left for Turkey. Returning towards the end of the year. Will be great to get together soon. Have a lovely festive season. Cheers for now. Enes'

'Oh, wow you are in Turkey. I am soooo jealous!!!! Okay cool lets connect when you get back. Hope you're having an awesome time.'

'Such nice mild chilly weather…enjoying it. I am here for my nieces wedding which is tonight. Let's see how it goes…'

That had gone really well, I thought. He was open, welcoming and friendly and seemed really pleased to hear from me. I was excited!

*Would anything have happened if I had not sent this first message? I will never know. Would it have changed anything? Would he have contacted me? When you are dealing with a self professed, emotionally unavailable man it probably makes no difference whatsoever whether you made the first move or not. He is not thinking along the lines of relationship, remember? As a general rule of thumb, I don't really agree with my son. Perhaps it is outdated but men still have it in their DNA to hunt you down and drag you into their cave, if they're attracted to you. On the other hand, men are only human and may also want to know that you're as interested as they are. If you have good self esteem and truly believe you have nothing to lose then go for it, but if this man has already warned you that he is unavailable for relationship then bear this in mind and know that if you do fall for him, it is going to be a 'bump-a-dee-bump' ride or perhaps no ride at all.*

## 20th December - Monday

I only sent a reply today…

'Hey a friend pooped in and I only got to see your reply later. Must be so cool to have some chilly weather after Jo'burg heat waves. Hope the wedding was loads of funnnn.'

I quickly sent another one…'Oops that was supposed to be popped.'

'Hehe sweet. We had a very good time last night. Trying to recover now.'

'Okay well have a lovely chilled day.'

A family wedding photo came through of him with the bride and groom and a couple of other people and an older woman, I assumed must be his mother. This I thought was a really positive sign, him sharing a family moment.

'Cool family photo…is that your mom? Have you recovered? Where in Turkey are you?'

'Yes, that's mom. I am ok now…just did a long walk. The outskirts of Ankara…a lovely peaceful suburb.'

'I will have to check that out on a map. Have a lovely evening.'

(I later felt a bit embarrassed when I found out that Ankara is actually the capital of Turkey. I had just assumed it was Istanbul, which historically, it was until the resistance moved its headquarters to Ankara during the British invasion).

This was my opportunity to really test the waters. I had made contact so I guess I should have left it there and given him the opportunity to show me that he was really interested but hey, people send New Year messages to each other all the time…no harm in just sending him another message…

*This is how women talk themselves out of their gut level intuitions all the time! I should probably have not sent this next message. Did I know that I was playing with fire - no of course I didn't, but perhaps if I had just breathed through the temptation to have more contact,*

> *I would not have spent the next six months of my life wondering if this man was into me or not. I will never know what the outcome would have been.*
>
> *Allow a man who is truly into to you, to let you know that he is. If he's not, then is a pursuit from your side really worth your time and effort? How will it serve your future relationship with this person in the long run? I did what I did and I guess this next message wasn't really responsible for making or breaking what would come to pass in the future but there is no harm in rather holding the energy and waiting....*

## January

### 2nd January - Saturday

I decided, 'Fuck it', and sent him a New Year message saying I hoped he was having a great holiday season and best wishes for the year ahead. He reciprocated with well wishes and asked when I was free to connect — were week days suitable or weekends better? I replied that I didn't have a nine-to-five job so either way was good for me. He apologised for not being in touch sooner but had been doing some *cleansing* for the New Year. He said we must get together for a chat over coffee and would be in touch in the next week.

I'm really excited to see him again.

## February

### 18th February - Thursday

Time seems to be flying by so quickly and it's already well into the new year. I was quite disappointed that Enes didn't follow through on the plans to get together. So much for me placing an expectation on it and thinking that he seemed really interested in seeing me again.

> **Getting to know an emotionally unavailable man will be a gradual process. Ask yourself if you have that amount of time, patience and dedication to allow him whatever time he needs and even if you do, will the end result be what you had been hoping for? If you are a busy girl with your own career commitments, a full social calendar and are able to keep your emotions in check through long waits with no real result in sight, then go for it at your own peril.**

Dona invited me over for dinner tonight. I've been seeing quite a bit of her since she left Steve (her long term partner) and moved closer to me. I must say, it's been nice to have a girl friend who's not too far away. We got chatting about our conversation to go to Turkey and I mentioned that I really should have a get together and invite Enes over. She suggested that I just invite him for lunch with a couple of people - *What did I have to lose?* I thought to myself, '*Only my heart*' but didn't say that to her. I don't want anybody to know how terrified I am to live through another broken hearted story and especially now when I'm in recovery. She has been in a long term partnership. Her relationship experience is different to mine. She's never been in and out of relationships that didn't develop into something lasting - and I doubt that she could relate in any real experiential way, to how tired and damaged I feel from all the years of pain — just too many deaths and relationship abandonments in my past. Putting myself out there again is a biggie - it's definitely not a case of, 'I've got nothing to lose'. But I do know I still have resources. I've always been a courageous woman, able to stretch myself beyond my fears — but at the same time, I am really scared to visit that place again with a man.

# 19ᵗʰ February - Friday

I decided to send Enes a message. I would keep it general in nature and tell him I had visited Dona and we got chatting about our plan to make new friends. I didn't want him to know how much I wanted to see him again and I didn't want him to feel like I was coming on to him. I asked him if he was free on Sunday for lunch or if it was too short notice, maybe the next weekend. I said I would keep it small. I knew I was using the, *Dona and I got talking,* line as a copout but I thought it would make him feel more comfortable and me less vulnerable.

He came back to me apologising for not following through on his previous arrangement. He had been sick with a stomach thing and it had knocked him. He said he had a birthday lunch to go to but how about dinner on Tuesday night in my area.

Wow, finally a set day and plan to get together. I suggested a place called the Greek Sizzler that had outside seating and a nice vibe. His reply was that he would be more comfortable doing something at my place.

I said I didn't mind cooking and he could invite his eccentric friend if he wanted to. He replied that his friend was away but I was still welcome to invite my friend. I was in two minds about inviting her. I am extremely nervous and the thought of being alone with him is really intimidating but on the other hand, I do really want him all to myself. My fear got the better of me and I invited her. She was, after all, my long term friend and she was in support of me. I thought of her as a type of *chaperone*...

He came back to me asking if I liked Sushi? I said Sushi sounded like a wonderful idea. He said no need to cook then, he would bring dinner.

I'm really beside myself excited to see this man again but filled with anxiety at the same time. It's such a long time since I had a man around.

## 23rd February - Tuesday

Enes arrived first, with a large platter of sushi in hand and a punnet of strawberries. So sweet. We sat on the patio chatting easily – I felt completely relaxed and at ease in his company. He loved my place and said, "This is your place". He knew I had only been there a short time. I almost regretted inviting Dona and even regretted it more when she arrived. I had dressed down because it was dinner at home. I didn't want to appear over dressed. I looked good but I was casually dressed. Dona arrived looking like she had spent the entire afternoon, dressing for a *sizzling hot date*. In all the years I have known her, I don't think I have ever seen her looking so *preened*. I quickly realised that she had not come here to support me and be my *wing woman* - she had come to make an impression on the man I was hoping to develop something with.

She joined us on the patio. I had made some yummy vegetable snacks with dips. Enes asked her what she did for a living and she told him that she ran a promotions company. Dona was actually struggling financially so whatever it was she was doing, wasn't really working. Her long term boyfriend had supported her financially and kept her afloat for years. She told us about a meditation evening that she would be starting up soon and Enes told her he would come. I already knew that I probably wouldn't go - I pretty much felt that many of these little gatherings were *pseudo spiritual*. Group meditating, with the 'I'm oh so spiritual' wasn't my thing but I didn't want to express any judgement and didn't say anything.

Fortunately I felt empowered and put myself in the position of an observer as I watched Dona fluff her feathers around this fine Turkish man. A thought crossed my mind - all she can see are dollar signs in her own future. I don't know why, I didn't really feel threatened. I watched him and her, engaging a little bit more than I would have liked. I watched as she crossed her legs on my sprawling couch and sensually pushed her skirt down between her legs, coyly and obviously, to hide her panties. I watched them both and still I didn't feel threatened - perhaps because I sensed he wasn't really that interested but I did pick up that he had clearly noticed. What normal man, would not? I think what she hadn't realised, was that Enes wasn't just an ordinary man with a small, one sided brain and as the watcher, this dawned on me – he was different. Most men would have been secretly salivating. This made me like him even more. I felt comforted by his presence - safe. He was solid, perhaps more of a real man than any man I had ever met – according to my perception of what that meant.

He even tried to take a look at my noisy fridge because it was bothering me. When last has any man tried to look at anything of mine, with a view to wanting to help? He reminded me a bit of the man my father would have been, had he not liked the sound of his own voice so much. Enes wasn't quiet but he was also a listener. I liked his balance.

He and Dona left the same time because he said he only knew the dirt roads in the area and she said she was driving on the better tar roads. I got the feeling she thought, this meant he actually fancied her because he didn't choose to stay longer, alone with me. I thought this was a possibility but a bigger part of me felt like I had nothing to worry about.

I came inside and landed into my comfy lazy boy where Enes had sat. I wasn't blown away by fireworks but I noticed I felt extremely centred and grounded. His presence in my home had felt wholesome. I like him a lot!

## 24ᵗʰ February - Wednesday

I woke up this morning feeling all warm and fuzzy about last night, as I realised that Enes is very discernible from any man I have ever known before. Perhaps with him I could break my historical pattern of dysfunctional men, and finally have something wholesome in my life. It felt like there could be real potential for a relationship with him. I decided to message him and thank him for bringing the food. He did, after all, bring the sushi and the strawberries - showing thanks and appreciation was the right thing to do.

He replied that he had enjoyed the time at my awesome place and the company, *'Thank you. See you again soon!'*

Later that evening I got a message from him. He had found the English version of the book he had been telling me about, when we were out on the patio, before Dona arrived - about a woman who walked across Australia with Aborigines. He asked me for my email address so he could send it to me. Wow, I was completely blown away by this. In the old days, when I was still in the dating arena, this would all point to us seeing each other again, really soon. It was all sounding positive and I had strong feeling I had met a man who is interested in developing something deeper than just a friendship, with me. *'How awesome would that be?'* I thought, *'It would change my life - my entire existence. I must keep myself in check,'* I reminded myself, *'This is amazing but really scary at the same time'.*

## 25ᵗʰ February - Thursday

I messaged Enes to let him know I got the message and didn't want to disturb him late. I thanked him and sent my email address. He later messaged back to say it had been sent. I received the book, *Mutant Messages from Down Under* by Marlo Morgan. I sent an email reply to say thanks again. I also mentioned the cosy, rainy weather and how much I enjoy the smell of wet earth wafting through my window - I could sense the plants sighing with relief to finally feel the rain. I said we must get together soon.

## 26ᵗʰ February - Friday

He sent an email back saying it had been a misty morning and it was lovely staying at home weather – then just before my heart started singing - he wished me a good weekend. Of course this pretty much meant that he didn't have any intention of visiting over the weekend. I was disappointed. The weekend was the perfect opportunity for us to spend more time getting to know each other.

I went to the plot to visit the twins. (My son, Lucien and his wife Katz live close by with my twin grandsons, of fifteen months, who I visit often on weekday afternoons) I love our visits. I took them for a walk. It was also an excuse to get some exercise and give their nanny a break. We chased butterflies and sang *Five Little Ducks*. I sing this song with them often and do the actions for *wiggle waggle, wiggle waggle* all in a row. I'm sure it's not very sexy but hey, nobody I want to impress is watching. We hugged trees and it's so cute to see their little arms around a tree trunk as they give it a big hug. I'd like to instil in them, an awareness of the energetic connection between us and nature.

## 28ᵗʰ February - Sunday

I printed out the book and spent the whole day on my bed reading. How did Enes know that I would totally relate to this book – the questioning of Western values and how they have destroyed all the cultures of the *real people* of the world. I wondered what he had been up to over the weekend and I wondered, even harder, why he hadn't made a plan to see me.

I sent him a message this evening letting him know that I had spent the whole day reading my new book and how much I was loving it. I asked him how his weekend had been. He replied that had had been out jogging and had just got home and had spent time at a home makers expo with his friend who had a stall there - the thought crossed my mind - *perhaps he's gay – all the best men seem to be gay*. I guess it was just because he wasn't following the usual, predictable, expected next step in the dating process. It's becoming clear that there is nothing predictable about this man and that I have a lot to learn about him and what makes him tick.

*Your emotionally unavailable crush will not slot into any behaviour that you deem to be a given. He is a law unto himself. Only he knows why he does or doesn't do what he does. You are unlikely to know what he's thinking or feeling because he is unlikely to offer you his thoughts. He may be prepared to tell you if you ask but you will sense that asking him directly may just push him to go and hang his hat at the entrance of somebody else's dinner table. And besides, why would you be entitled to*

> *this information – he hasn't given you any indication that you are a welcome guest.*

### 29ᵗʰ February - Monday

I decided not to reply immediately to his message – maybe I shouldn't be so available all the time? I replied when I got back from visiting my grandsons and sent him a picture of them. He said they were such cute kids. I would love him to meet them. I have a sore throat and not feeling great on any level. I want to see this man again. Sore throats indicate not expressing oneself – daaah – what am I supposed to say – why are you being so avoidant? Yeah, right and have him heading for the hills.

### 31ˢᵗ February – Wednesday

I got a message from Dona today to invite me to her new meditation group and asking me to invite Enes as well. She seems to have gotten this group together very quickly. She had been talking about it for months and now suddenly within a week, it's happening - another red flag that she really does fancy him. Do I have a right to feel some form of betrayal from my so called friend? Of course she believes that her invitation is coming across as perfectly ingenuous and has no idea that I can see right through her.

I have a serious dilemma about this. I don't want to go and the last thing I want is for Enes to go alone without me, but I do not own him and he did express an interest in going. I wish I could just tell my friend to keep her hands off my new *crush*. Can't she just be happy for me instead of trying to worm her way in? I know he's a catch - that's why I like him so much. The night we met, he came to me and asked me for my number. She was also there. He didn't ask her for hers. Now she was putting me on the spot. I had a right to a *checking it out* phase without sharing him – having him go and integrate with her and her friendship circle. I had never nudged myself inappropriately into to her life before. I know this sounds like teenage stuff but I *really* like this man and I *really* don't want him to go to the meditation group without me. I will go if I *have to go* but I am going to do my best to avoid it.

I decided to phone my son and run it by him. What was I going to do? He told me that I had to let him know. If he found out that he had been invited and I hadn't told him, it would not be cool. I agreed. I needed to stay in integrity. There was nothing I could do if he was actually attracted to her. I had to prepare myself for this possibility. I couldn't rule that out so I had to find a way to let him know and give him the option but at the same time, leave it open for me to decide whether or not I was going to go. I typed the message being very mindful of how I worded it…

*'Helllooo…Dona has sent me info about the meditation group she is having tomorrow night and said I must let you know. I don't know if I am up for a group mediation thing but will see how I feel tomorrow. I will forward you the info if you're keen to go. I know that you expressed an interest. Let me know and I will send you the details.'*

He replied that he might go but would also see how he feels tomorrow and thanked me. I replied that he must come around again for dinner soon and he was always welcome to come and spend some time in the peace of the countryside. We sent a few messages backwards and forwards about my swimming activities and what we were both up to in general. I am passionate about swimming and I'm so blessed to have this lovely pool on the property. I really enjoy doing my lengths which I wanted to share with him…nice positive stuff that doesn't include any further conversation about going meditating around my flirty friend. I *really* didn't want him to say he had decided to go. I am just holding it together but inside, my vulnerable, insecure woman is freaking out.

# March

## 2nd March - Wednesday

I heard my phone beep after two. I breathed before I read the message. He asked how I was and said he couldn't make it, unfortunately. I smiled a big 'YAY' and sighed with relief — how fortunate. Now he wouldn't have her details and it pretty much confirmed that he was not after her *'bod'* otherwise he would have grabbed the opportunity to see her again. I replied, casually, that I also wasn't going. I told him I was going to visit the twins and would have a swim when I got home and then just chill out. I was *soooo* relieved. The potential with this man was growing in my mind.

## 6ᵗʰ March - Sunday

My previous delight has turned into withering deflation - four days since the last message. I was praying he was going to make that next move — the one that confirms, *I'm so distractedly into you, nothing can hold me back.* A message came through this morning. He was just asking how I am but I was incredibly elated to hear from him - like he was inviting me to elope with him to Turkey. I didn't reply straight away - I have this thing - when a message comes through, I wait to read it. I think it's partly *angst* that he may actually make a move and it's partly *panic* that he won't — the time of waiting is like hovering in a safety zone, between knowing he's made contact and the not knowing exactly what that means. I know this sounds absurd and I'm not exactly sure why I do it — all I know is I like leaving it *hanging* in the air, like a little iridescent soap bubble, prancing around before it pops. He replied that he was thinking of a quick visit but he had lunchtime plans and felt it was a bit too late now. Aaaah, if only I had known - but I actually had plans of my own. I replied that I was going to Jo'burg to have lunch with a friend then visiting someone to chat about a book translation. It's good to let him know I also have a life, right? I don't often *have a life* but today I did. He also mentioned that his electricity had been off for a while so I commented on how crappy that was.

I went off to town to have lunch with my friend at a quaint Portuguese Restaurant. Afterwards I had plans to visit my long ago ex, Khyle, who I have asked to translate my little romance novella into German. I was rather taken aback when I saw him. He's suffering from dementia and looks so incredibly weather beaten for his age. It's really hard to imagine how in love with him

I was - how I had been convinced that he was my twin flame, the love of my life - but that was so long ago now. I realised during that visit, there was no way he could possibly do the translation. I doubted he could even read it properly. It was awfully sad.

Enes messaged me later on in the evening to say that his power had only just come back on - South Africa is really going down the tubes fast. We had an awesome messaging flow going on and I'm now convinced that I will definitely see him again soon. I may just have landed myself a potential boyfriend. Wouldn't that just be frigging amazing! It felt really good.

## 9ᵗʰ March - Wednesday

The last few days, I have been reminding myself to take it easy with having false expectations around who I think this man is to me. It's so easy to project and place an agenda on this connection I feel to him. It's been three days since our last message and I'm wondering if it would be okay to make the next move. Since the dinner, I have largely been waiting to hear from him first. I know it's not a game of chess - not every move has to be calculated but in my past, I never had to reach out to men – I always waited for them to show very clear signs of interest in me, but my romantic past is so long ago now. It feels like a lifetime ago or even another person's life. It almost feels like I am doing this for the very first time and I have absolutely no clue how to do it.

*When you are falling for an emotionally unavailable man you often find yourself feeling perplexed. You doubt yourself and may even doubt your attractiveness because he does not view woman in terms of their potential as a mate – or at least pretends not to, either to just you or himself as well. This can make you feel, almost androgynous – he could be relating to you as a woman but you get the feeling you could just as well be a man friend to him. At this point, a man who is interested will probably be a bit more flirty. He is testing the waters just as much as you are. The distance*

> *that an emotionally unavailable man keeps between you can be very confusing because it is neither here nor there. Is he shy? Is it hot or cold? Is it on or off? Nothing is clear as you look for signs or try to fathom it out by reading between the lines.*

It's all drizzly and overcast today, a welcome break from the dryness. It's snugly weather and my mind wonders over to how amazing it would be to have someone to curl up next to – under warm blankets with *body heat* and a good movie or two to watch together. For the longest time I didn't think about intimate moments but now I long to rest my head, furled up on a strong shoulder, in the enclave of a man's arms. I decide what harm can a message do? I sent a message saying how much I was loving the cosy weather (a very cryptic hint) and asked how he was doing.

He replied later to say he had just arrived home and could now enjoy it after a busy day and getting up at 2:30 in the morning for work and was exhausted. He also expressed that he liked the emoticons I always include in my messages. He said I must be a visual person. That really makes me smile inside. I replied that I have always been a creative person and enjoy painting so I must be. I told him that I am able to visualise events very clearly in my mind - that's why I am able to translate detail into my writing. I also said that it was the perfect night for snuggling under covers and told him to enjoy his early night. I would have revelled in being more flirty with him and asked if he felt like having somebody over to *get it on with* but that would have perhaps come across as too pushy or presumptuous. Once again, lovely chats backwards and forwards about warm houses and his cat who hasn't left the heater. It all flowed so nicely and I am, once again, feeling really positive about him – he seems to have a very demanding work life.

I have plans to go away with Dona for the weekend and now I am wishing I hadn't committed to it. She had mentioned that I could invite Enes if I wanted to and of course that isn't going to happen. The last thing I need is a *whole weekend* of watching her trying to get her claws into him and his bank account. I would cancel if I could but I have already paid. Besides, there is a whole crowd going for an adventure to the countryside and it may be just what I need to get out of my head and my fantasies about spending time with the elusive Enes. I have never been to the little town of Groot Mariko and I am always up for exploring new places. A part of me felt like I should let Enes know - why - I had no idea. I didn't owe him an explanation. He wasn't really in my life yet and there was no harm in him believing I have my own *happening* life, which does not include him at this point - even though I would have dropped everything for him if he had said the word. He was the person I wanted to spend time with - I knew this already. I really had no interest in being a lonely, inconsequential face in the crowd anymore.

*A relationship with an emotionally unavailable man can appear to be On, followed by an Off. It can truly be as fickle as the flip of a light switch – the light goes on and you feel it's brightness - the light goes off and you're left in the dark, not forgetting that this one also has a dimmer – bright, dark, dim, dark, bright, dim, dark, dark, dim, bright – Got it? The moments of light will be few and far between. Best you get a back up torch to shine a light on the other aspects of life that make you feel fulfilled and happy.*

## 13th March - Sunday

I have just landed back from my weekend in Groot Mariko. I didn't have signal the whole weekend and wondered whether Enes had tried to message me. On the way back, I switched my phone on, praying I would be greeted by an outreach from him. There was nothing. My heart sank into my shoes. My hope that there would be continuity - that he wanted me in his life just as much as I wanted him - that he was just busy - that he was just taking it slow, was evaporating, leaving a mushy, soggy lump of crumpled disappointment.

The weekend away had made me feel more alienated than before I left. I felt completely disconnected. It was a realisation that I am changed - that who I have become and what I aspire to be is quite apart from the majority. I have always known this, but I had also always been able to find people, quite easily, who I could resonate with. This group of people seemed strangely mismatched - they were not resonating with each other and I felt completely removed and isolated from the experience.

There was one man, the extremely tall lanky, Jay who had held out his hand to me to help me over a rock as we traversed the hiking trail, with whom I felt a *likeness of being*. I remembered him from parties, festivals and drumming circles many years ago but it was really like meeting him for the first time. He was also not drinking and said he had given up any form of drugs, including weed so we kind of related on that level but at the same time, he was easy to talk to and be around. To be honest, I quite like him but I don't know if I can LIKE, LIKE him like I LIKE Enes.

He was pretty keen on me travelling back with him but the couple he brought down with him didn't offer to sit in the enclosed back of his truck so we exchanged numbers and said we would be in touch. It may be nice to have a *buddy* to do stuff with if Enes doesn't come through for me. I'm feeling pretty down in the dumps about him not messaging me - I *really* want it to be him. *I really, really LIKE him, Like him.*


## 15ᵗʰ March - Tuesday

Lisa came to visit me and mentioned how terrible it was about the bombing in Ankara. I didn't even know about it. I decided it was a good excuse to message Enes seeing as his family live there. I messaged him, later on that night, to say that I had been away for the weekend and had no signal or had heard no news. My friend popped in for a visit and told me about the bombing... I hoped his family were all okay. He came back, five minutes later, to say that it was great that I could get away like that. He had been busy with training at work. He said his family was fine and these incidents happened and then passed by. He then told me that he had sent me another book earlier. A man who has not been thinking about you doesn't purchase and send you books, including a link to an E-book reader to download. Oh wow, my mood shifts from non-descript to ecstatic in an instant.

I'm beginning to notice that we have a lot of synchronicity going on, almost like we somehow read each other's thoughts. Perhaps he had felt the gap and this was his way of making contact – a book is a nice way of telling someone you care about them. I went to check my email and there was nothing so I messaged to tell him there was no book from him.

## 16ᵗʰ March – Wednesday

I got a message from Enes first thing this morning to say he must have sent it to the wrong address. He forwarded it and I could see that he had made an attempt to send it to another woman with my first name. I wonder if he was trying to locate my book and trying another email address of an author he'd found. He knew I wrote under a pseudonym. I opened the book by an author who shared my surname. Other books by this author included a book on the art of seduction - Mmmnnn, I wonder if he bought that one too – I couldn't help but think that perhaps he was planning a seduction. *'Maybe he's insecure'*, I told myself and I really shouldn't give up on this guy too soon. I honestly don't care too much how this man performs or doesn't perform in bed. What I have already seen about him tells me enough to want him in my life, regardless of his physical prowess. I was looking for expansion, and a deep connection, not perfection.

I find it interesting that this writer and I share the same surname and the person he wrongly emailed had my first name - I strongly suspect he was being a *pen name detective*, and searching for my book. That would mean this guy is very intrigued by the mystery of who I am as an author.

I downloaded the book reader from the link Enes had sent me and skimmed the book. I could immediately tell that I wasn't going to enjoy it nearly as much as the first one he sent me. The book was about people who have mastered their craft and a *how to* on reaching mastery in your own life. It was an interesting topic and I could see how Enes would have thought it would appeal to me. He did say that he hadn't read it yet. What I did love about the book, was that Enes had reached out to me with it. It could have been a book about vacuum cleaners for all I cared - it was the gesture that spoke volumes. He cared enough about me to look for and buy a book he thought I would enjoy. Surely this meant he values me and our connection? And so begins our new form of long distance, deeper communication - more emailing. I sent him a thank you and said it had put a big smile on my face.

He replied telling me he had, had a hectic few days of intensive training at work. He had been getting up in the middle of the night to work and by the evening was totally exhausted. Shame the poor guy - and in the middle of all of this, he sends me a book. Wow! He said he's looking forward to the coming long weekend, where he will have time to get some things done and will also make time to see me. Enes was going to make time to see me! I re-read it just to make sure - *Enes is going to make time to see me!* Now I really have something to look forward to - no set plans but I would see him some time over the long weekend.

## 17ᵗʰ March - Thursday

Enes sent me an email about how our organs carry cellular memory and we must talk to them. I love the fact that he shares insights with me - and I am very aligned with this idea. I have always believed in the mind-body connection and believe in affirmations to clear mental patterns that create *dis-ease* in our bodies. I've done some reading about cellular memory and I am fascinated by the documented accounts of how people, who receive donor organs, can take on the likes and dislikes of the donor - things that they would never have connected with in their past.

There doesn't seem to be enough space in cell messages to share all we have to share so we are resorting more and more to deeper and longer sharing in emails. I emailed back and agreed that I do believe in cellular memory. The thought crossed my mind about a pact I had made with myself, after being on a dating site, many years ago, and establishing a long distance email connection with a guy who dumped me for another woman, by simply just ignoring me. We had been writing, every day, for three months. I had shared and poured so much of myself out to him. I vowed I would never do this again - and there's a big difference. He was actually long distance. He lived on a boat in Hout Bay harbour in Cape Town. But the long weekend is approaching, with a promise of seeing Enes in real time - and I am beside myself, keyed up for our second face to face date - well, perhaps more like hang out time - we shall see.

## 17ᵗʰ March – Thursday

I went shopping to find my daughter-in-law, Katz, a birthday present. She mentioned, a while ago, that she wants to do photo albums for the boys. I didn't realise how difficult it would be to find decent albums and it was a lot of leg work but I eventually found one I really like. It took me the entire day but it feels good. I am healing and I have the energy and stamina now to do running around - very happy about that. I think I am recovered from my Pancreatitis. Perhaps my specialist was wrong and it isn't going to take six to nine months. Yay!

Enes messaged and I briefly shared the events of my day and my weekend plans. I have a lunch date with my son's in-laws on the public holiday, which falls on Monday, for Katz's birthday, and I wonder if it would be in any way appropriate to invite Enes. I would love to invite him but we haven't even spent our own time together and maybe it would seem too much like I'm thinking of him as a boyfriend. I decide it's better to wait. As much as I would love to include him, this is a family occasion with her family and it's not like I am close enough to them to include a *sort-of-ish*, maybe guy in my life.

## 20th March – Sunday

So, after my email to Enes, in reply to him saying that he would come over and see me over the long weekend - I responded by saying he could come over, have some dinner and watch a movie if he likes - Friday afternoon, we messaged then nothing… This morning I feel like a crumpled deflated, cold air balloon. It looks like Enes is letting me down. I run my old movie script through my mind about how I can't handle another failed relationship and wonder what the hell I think I'm doing? I can't go down this old, tyre worn out track again. I know exactly where it ends. It feels like hell. I want a relationship, particularly with this man but I'm not sure I have the stamina or resources to go through these ghastly, uncertain beginning stages. He's just so elusive and intangible - and now finally, after weeks of patiently waiting, he is showing his true colours – he's letting me down!

## *Later*

Lisa messaged me to ask if I wanted to meet her at a craft market in the country. I didn't feel like getting dressed, let alone going out but agreed to go. I just wanted to curl up in a ball and feel sorry for myself in peace - I don't think I can handle anymore knocks. If this is what one little rejection, with a man I'm not even involved with, feels like, imagine how I would feel if I got into a relationship with him - and he walked out on me? It scares the hell out of me! What the F#@* was I thinking? How could I even have dreamed I could do this? I assumed he was also scared, for reasons only he could fathom, but if I could move through my fears then so could he!

I decided, '*What am I going to do, sitting around at home all day, with all this old, dishevelled baggage dragging me into a pit of putrid pessimism?*' I threw on my flowing hippie, tie dyed, turquoise dress, the one I had bought at the little stall on the boardwalk that overlooked the translucent turquoise sea in Turkey - added my colourful, purple, red and yellow bone necklace to make it pop, even though *popping* didn't exactly reflect my mood - grabbed my bag, scrambled into my car and headed for the market.

'*There see, look how easy that was*', I told myself. Now I was on my way, I decided to do something about my tangled hair and thought a bit of make-up may hide my dreary outlook on this day out. I felt like shit when I left home. I didn't give a damn about how I looked – I just needed to get myself out – but the reality was that I did actually care – maybe it was for the best – for my own good - if he exits my life now then I don't have to face a more devastating desertion in the future.

When I arrived, Lisa said I looked radiant. I felt far from anything remotely resembling radiant — more like redundant - but it was good to hear it, all the same. We sat around chatting with friends for a couple hours then at around five, Enes messaged me. How was my Sunday afternoon going? Shew, that had been a close call. This was his last chance to follow through on seeing me — he was walking a fine line — time was ticking between now and tomorrow!

I replied, *"I'm at a market. Phone battery about to die."* It wasn't a lie — and I was grateful for the little empty symbol on my dying phone. What was I supposed to say, *'I've been waiting to hear from you all day…I am so stoked over you, I can't breathe'.*

I needed a moment to assimilate! I had already made up my mind that he was a *no show*.

Lisa's house was just down the road so I decided to go over there and put my phone on charge and make a decision. My panic stricken, scared little girl wanted to back out and push him away - how could he expect me to be available at such short notice? Was he going to expect me to jump when he says jump?

Lisa suggested that I cut the guy some slack and invite him over for dinner. I wasn't ready for it. I had made no emotional or physical preparations for being put on the spot, with an ad lib dinner - but one thing I am quite confident about is my cooking ability, especially for a vegetarian. I was after all, a single mother, who raised two children on a shoestring and one of them had been a vegetarian - I knew exactly how to make simple but tasty food at a moment's notice.

I messaged him to say I was at a friend's house having tea and charging my phone… and heading home soon. What was he up to?

He was at his friend's house, down the road from me and could he come over for tea? I replied that I could whip us up something to eat and he replied, cool he would bring over some organic, home grown veggies from his friend's little organic farm.

I smoked a couple of *real* cigarettes. I had a knot in my stomach the size of a rugby ball and was extremely anxiously excited. Was I mad to be doing this? I left. On my way home, I realised that I had just run out of the house and it was not in any state for a visit from a potential boyfriend. Was I insane? What had possessed me to invite him over? My dustbin needed emptying - my fridge needed clearing out. He called - how much longer? I told him I was about ten minutes away.

I charged into the house and scooped out the dustbin bag, which was smelly and overdue and chucked some leftover food from my fridge into it - grabbed some cushions to scatter on my newly painted bench on the patio. The dogs started barking. I ignored them, knowing full well he was already at the gate. Then I called him – unavailable - then I went to the gate to see him reversing out. I called him again. He answered. I told him I was waiting for him at the gate. I let him in, realising that I hadn't even rinsed the aftermath of the cigarette smoke from my mouth. We hugged hello and then a big basket of organic veggies came marching towards my front door.

"My house isn't as perfect as the first time you were here," I admitted coyly.

He said he would stand outside and wait if there were things I needed to do - I ushered him inside. As he walked inside he said, *"It's perfect to me"* - who says stuff like that? I am reminded of why I like him so much. He is kind - he is solid, he is a real man.

He unpacks vegetables on to my kitchen counter, the ones he is donating to me and for our dinner tonight. I tell him they look so beautiful; the tomatoes look like works of art - they are the sectioned variety that look like little pumpkins but are bright red. They are so red they almost look unnatural. Nothing you buy from a supermarket ever looks like this - they were oozing freshness and wholesomeness.

We sit on the patio, sipping grape juice. How different it is not to have alcohol to ease the newness angst but I notice that there is really no angst. He is impressed with the fresh paint on the bench and tells me, *"You're handy, huh'.* I reply, *'It's called being a single mom'.*

He tells me that he has been trying to overcome Adrenal Fatigue. It drains him and he can't plan ahead. He explains that he never knows how he is going to feel on any given day. I tell him that I can totally relate. I was still recovering from the Pancreatitis and my energy levels also didn't allow me to have that *get up and go* feeling and I also struggled to plan ahead.

I told him that I wasn't going to go, the day we met and I still don't actually know why I went - how I really didn't feel like going but that I had pushed myself. *"Ad lib is much better"* he says. He is reliable so he would rather not make a commitment. He doesn't like breaking his word.

I think of telling him about one of my favourite quotes from the book, A Course In Miracles, *'Today I make no decisions, I forgot what to decide'*. For some reason, I don't. We agree about not planning ahead. I tell him I'm going to make some food now so we should move inside. He says he doesn't need much.

I get to the kitchen and know exactly what to cook for this man. I make a kick ass Lentil Rice with butter fried onions and tons of garlic. With that, I can make a Turkish Dip with yogurt, dried mint (that I actually bought in Turkey) and garlic. I have falafel mix, which makes the most yummy falafel balls.

Now I have a man sitting on my sleeper couch, leaning against cushions looking straight into my open plan kitchen. I have my back to him because the kitchen counter runs along the edge of the tiled wall so I am gathering up the ingredients, for an ad lib first time cooking dinner, with a guy I have the *'hots'* for. Under normal circumstances, a glass or two of wine would have gone down nicely in this scenario. It would have completely taken the edge off but strangely, I do not feel as intimidated as I would have imagined, especially seeing as, after rummaging around in my kitchen cupboard, I cannot find Lentils and that means I have to re-imagine my rice dish - no problem, I will make *'flied lice'* so I put the rice on to cook. It will give me an opportunity to use more of the organic veggies that had miraculously materialised on my kitchen counter.

All this time, I am pausing and turning around to engage in conversation. He tells me about his friend who stayed with him who had Pancreatitis and how he had no appetite and lost so much weight. Now my suspicions about him, perhaps being gay, surface. Is he hinting at this - a guy who stayed with him - his friend. Is he gay?

I am chopping onions, grating garlic and chopping freshly picked organic parsley, to fry up for the rice - I have some pre-cooked broccoli, which I add to the mix in the buttery pan. I pray he is not gay!

He tells me about his married friend who is cheating on his wife. He wonders how he thinks he can get away with this energetically. I am listening but it's nearly time to toss the rice into the mix and I have to get that dip on the go. He says something about it's not his inclination - at this point, that's all I hear -what's not his inclination?

I turn around and ask him directly, *"Don't you like woman? Are you gay?"*

He says he's not or something to that effect and I feel myself smiling inside, even though I am now mixing the dried mint into the yogurt and running outside to my patio to pluck a little bit of fresh mint from its pot. I throw in the rice - stir, stir, stir - realise it has no colour so I tell him it needs colour so I chop in one of those gorgeous red peppers which makes it look much more appetising then I beat an egg. He asks why I am adding egg. I forget he's a vegetarian and don't even ask if he eats egg —oops - all I say is, *"It's evolving"*. Rice is done. Now I can form the falafel balls that have been soaking in warm water, to fry. The consistency is perfect and I'm happy about that. They are sizzling at medium heat in the pan.

Dinner is about ready to serve. I look at the clock on the wall and realise I have been cooking for two hours. I make a joke about how long it's taken me. I set the table and produce some Chilli powder that I just so happen to have also bought in Turkey. I ask him how many people he knows can actually give him Turkish spices when he goes there for dinner? He says not many, not even Turkish people have Turkish spices. Once the food is on the table, it looks so sparse - did it really take me two hours to produce this? He takes his first couple of bites...

"This is delicious," he says.

My heart swells. I have to confess, my food is perfect. In fact, the Turkish dip is the best I've ever tasted and the best one I've ever made.

After dinner, he jokes about a *doggy bag* and I am more than happy to give him take home food - I love feeding people and I'm so happy that my *at a moment's notice* meal was such a success.

Now we have a chance to sit and chat. He tells me he had two six year relationships.

I joke and say, "So your cut off point is six years?"

"And that was pretty much six or seven years ago - he emphasises - *a real relationship!*"

Okay so that obviously does not exclude sex. He is not a monk or a reborn virgin like me.

At nine-thirty I tell him, *"It's your bedtime"* with a cheeky grin on my face.

He says, "Yes" but I can tell he's not yet ready to leave.

I tell him about my idea to bury my gall bladder stones with a letter to them – a little ritual to release them to say goodbye. I also mention the Louise Hay affirmation for Pancreas - *'Life is sweet and so am I'*. (I was told that gall bladder stones can fetch a good price from traditional healers but I'd much rather return them to the earth.)

*"It's a lack of joy. Do you know, that loneliness has become the fastest growing disease on the planet - loneliness is causing illness,"* He says.

We chat a while longer and then he says it's time to go. He leaves with a basket, now not so heavily laden, and a *doggie bag*. I walk him out into the moonlit night. We stand and admire the moon that hangs, halfway exposed, halfway hidden in the darkness of the country night sky. We hug, *noncommittally*, at his car door. We are like mirrors of this moon. Is the cup half empty or half full? We shall have to wait and see...

A feeling of *neutrality* or is it *shock* -  lasts for just a few minutes as I slump into the lazy boy to absorb the evening with Enes – moments of respite before my heart realises that it's opening and awakening to this beautiful solid, Turkish man. I am then overwhelmed with delight and elation. This is the beautiful side of the cellular memory of being with a man intimately - the nights of slow love making, being held, rocked in a soft, warm cradle and in that moment, I want that again - specifically with this man. If I wasn't completely available before, I am now making myself available (this I do sub-consciously). I wonder if this man and I will go there. Tonight we opened up a space - the universe holds its breath - what will happen next? Let go, let go, it sighs. Everything is going to be alright...

*Always listen to what a man has to say to you - don't just listen, 'hear him'. I realise as I transfer this from my journal that I didn't really listen to what he was saying. He would try to do his best but he wasn't making me any promises - whether or not he was using his Adrenal Fatigue as a 'cop out' from making commitments, is not the 'issue' - he was telling me something - let's see later in the journal how this information could have benefited me, by accepting the reality, had I made a point of 'hearing him'.*

*I didn't yet know, that Enes was seriously and committed to being an emotionally unavailable man - and neither did I know what that really meant.*

Tonight I slip under the covers with a feeling of love expanding in my solar plexus. I lie, sleepless in a warm glow. I know I met Enes for a reason.

## 21ˢᵗ March Monday (public holiday)

A friend of mine reminded me the other day about how your heart opens up when you fall in love. You walk around with a lightness of being - an openness and an all embracing feeling for life and the people around you. It's as if nothing or no-one can touch you negatively when you are in that space. The *so-called* more spiritually enlightened, will tell you that you can reach this state without projecting that feeling on to another - I don't know about that - perhaps you can, perhaps you can't - all I know is I woke up feeling incredibly good about myself, especially after Enes messaged me.

*'Thank you for the lovely time and awesome food…will eat the rest for breakfast just now…enjoy the party!!*

I notice how he separates his sentences with pause dots. I wonder how many people do that. I do it a lot!

## Later

I had such an awesome day today — that feeling I was talking about when your heart expands because you feel a love connection with someone. It's like you carry that person with you even though they aren't there. I am brimming over with *feel good energy*. I express my positivity in a message to him, being careful not to go overboard - just to tell him about my day. I also tell him how some people had been shocked that I was the twin's grandmother and not their mom. I told him it was good for my ego. He says it's the truth. I look too young to be a gran. He's so sweet. We have a lovely, positive messaging session and I have no doubt that I will see him again soon. I really, really, really like this man!

## 22ⁿᵈ March - Tuesday

I send my late father a happy birthday message in my mind, *"Happy birthday Daddy!"* My son calls this morning to ask if him and the twins can come and have lunch with me because Katz is studying and he has the day off work. What a nice surprise. I am so excited. My life suddenly feels great. I have a new man in my life and my family have been showing up in my life, for a change. I wonder if my father set this up, on some level so that we could be together on his birthday - me and my three boys. I have Enes on my mind. I would love for him to meet my son.

My boys and I spend a lovely day together. We take the twins for a walk to the jungle gyms at the play area. I love this feeling of being a family in my home with them. My son is such a stunning person and the twins — well, they're just too adorable. I give them boots I bought for them the other day. They look too sweet in their little, fake leather ankle boots. My heart swells with a new seed germinating — perhaps I survived for a purpose. Would it be too presumptuous to believe that I can finally enjoy some peace and happiness — that it's my time now - to shine!

After they leave, my feeling of connectedness, with Enes, grows larger inside of me — that *'angsty'* rugby ball becomes a soft orb. I long to see him again really soon. I wonder if he feels the same and hope that I am not creating an *illusion* around this - it can happen so easily.

I send him a photo of the boys and tell him I had visitors today - and beautiful children energy in my home. As I get no immediate reply, I start doubting myself — perhaps being a grandmother is not the sexiest angle. I try to conjure up a plan to show him my sensual woman side, without being lascivious. I heard once that a man's ideal woman is a mother and a whore, rolled into one - he's seen the mother - maybe I can find a way of showing him my sexy side. I have a feeling he's not ready for that yet… still no reply.

More doubts creep in and I ask myself, *'Are you setting yourself up for failure by creating capacious desires — jumping too far ahead — perhaps I should apply some brakes and allow the manifestation to catch up, in reality. I don't even know what this is yet'.*

I think about all the runaway test runs I've put myself through over the last ten years — all the empty launch pads. *'Give it a chance to breathe'*, I tell myself, *'put some spaces around it'* - now I'm back pedalling on a bicycle. I wonder if he's thinking it's too much — *'Oh, shit I am so frigging bad at this!'* The fear has arrived, which moves me from feel good into a state of paranoia. *'Oh God, sometimes I'm my own worst enemy - am I going to sabotage this?'*

And I'm feeling, oh so, sexual again, after a long, long time of thinking perhaps I had left that woman, from the past, behind me. I'm masturbating again. Being around this beautiful man has got my juices flowing. I've still got it! Wow! Everything in this area, is still working just as it should. It will be like riding that bicycle – I'm sure I will just get on it and remember exactly how to push those pedals. I am projecting on to our first sexual encounter... still no reply.

It's now past his bedtime - I've already played out a successful outcome in my mind. I am already convinced that he's just as into me as I am into him, but in reality I have absolutely no idea what he's thinking or feeling.

*Spending time with your emotionally unavailable man can be greatly satisfying. It can be exciting being around him and it may feel mutually appealing from both sides. Those times spent together confirm why you feel the way you do about him. You assume that he must feel the same and he would definitely want more of that - why wouldn't he? Did he leave you with any promises? Did he tell you he would see you again on a certain date or time? The spaces between the times that you spend with your emotionally unavailable man and the much longer, lonelier times that you don't, always feel like an eternity of being left dangling in the unknown. Who knows when he will be back – not even he knows! And the ludicrous part is the more avoidant he is, the more longing it creates in you.*

## 23rd March - Wednesday

Enes sent a message this afternoon that my previous message to him had gone out of his head – is this a case of out of sight out of mind? Sometimes he is clearly not a first English language speaker – my message went out of his head? What type of excuse was that? It felt a bit odd and the story I tell myself is that perhaps he thinks I'm getting too close and he's backing off - he seems to have gone lukewarm.

I tell him that I was sitting on the bench on my patio with a pen in hand but I've got a bit of writers block at the moment. He replies that he has about six notebooks filled with ideas and wonders how to get these to a point of translating them into a book. I send a message back explaining the process I went through with writing The Other Side of My Reflection (although of course I'm not telling him the name yet) - he doesn't reply. The message is left hanging in the air and I have an uncomfortable feeling - something is up. I am reminded of lines from an old song from my childhood, *"What do you get when you fall in love – a guy with a pin to burst your bubble. That's what you get for all your trouble…I'll never fall in love again."*

I really don't want to lose this positive vibe I've been feeling about this man but the flow has been abruptly interrupted – and I have absolutely no idea what happened. I feel incredibly ill at ease and confused about it. We felt so close after the dinner and now I'm feeling a big, gaping divide.

*Looking back, this is the place where Enes started distancing himself. We went from two people who both seemed equally there to one person feeling completely bewildered by his lack of real presence in her life. A self esteemed woman would probably have just said, "Oh well, I am worthy of being loved so if this man is not interested then I'm moving on". I imagine now how differently I could have handled it. I could have just given it breathing space. I could have been more elusive and mysterious about my life. I didn't have to answer every message straight away.*

*When you get the sense that an emotionally unavailable man is backing off, there is nothing wrong with allowing him some breathing space. Let him roam around freely in the jungle, out there, like a feral cat that has no real home. You can't really tame a cat. They have a mind of their own and will not conform to your expectations. They are not a dog – they will not sit when you say sit and they will never be your utterly devoted best friend. They come to you for love and attention if and when they chose and only accept your attention on their terms.*

*Is this what you really want? Is this what you signed up for when you told yourself you had fallen for this man? No, I'm sure you expected more, much more. Well, are you going to sit around and wait or are going to go out there and look elsewhere for what you really want? The choice is yours.*

## 25ᵗʰ March - Friday (Good Friday)

The Easter weekend is upon us and there are no plans to see Enes – four days of no work commitments for him. Surely he would make a plan to see me if he was into me? This would be the perfect opportunity. It sucks that he hasn't said anything – what actually happened or didn't happen is a complete enigma to me. Was I crazy to think that he was a potential man in my life? Was I that off course?

It's two days since I heard from Enes and, to be honest, it seems extremely odd because that last message I sent him wasn't one of those closing off messages. It was quite open ended – one where you assume a reply is inevitable because you are in the middle of a *conversation*. I wonder if there is a bit of a language or understanding barrier - perhaps he had misinterpreted what I was saying - did I say something wrong?

I feel like I totally jumped ahead of myself. I am fatigued and exhausted today. I remind myself that I am still in recovery. I am still adjusting to a different diet. I am also draining myself with negative thoughts about Enes. Now I'm thinking that he is definitely not showing the same amount of enthusiasm as I am. *Maybe he's just not that into me* – this thought makes me feel like an absolute idiot. I thought I had grown wiser with age, *'How could I have been so stupid?'* I berate myself.

So I played out all the different scenarios with this man. I imagined, after our successful dinner, things would flow in a natural progression. We would message. We would make arrangements to see each other again. Why wouldn't we? It had all gone so well. It's not supposed to feel like climbing up a great big, exhausting hill. He would ask what I was doing over the Easter weekend - we would hook up. That's how I remember it going, when you meet somebody you really like and you pretty much know they like you too. That was the norm.

I feel like I'm spinning out of control on a merry-go-round but there is nothing very merry about it – more like a dog chasing and biting its own tail - ouch. It feels like I'm back at the beginning again, asking myself, *'Who makes the first move?'* I lectured myself for doing so much of the reaching out but then I am reminded about the books. Men don't just buy a woman E-books if they are not the least bit interested in them.

*You will find yourself searching for explanations around what happened or is happening with your emotionally avoidant man. Woman, generally, have a tendency to make up their own stories around what men could be thinking or feeling. With an emotionally unavailable man it is mostly your best guess – does he even know the answer to this question and if so, will he ever tell you – it's doubtful you will ever find out. It could be anything from you were getting too close and he's backing away or an acorn fell on his head and he's nursing a swollen bump. It could have something to do with you or nothing at all. Maybe he's just 'out there'*

> *exploring or 'in there' in his own little bubble, philosophising about the hidden meaning behind the fact that the acorn fell from the tree at that exact moment when he was passing by – yes, it will be a guessing game full of assumptions and reading between the lines - an utter waste of your precious time and energy.*

I remember having the feeling of not being scared of him anymore and I let my guard down - all that new relationship angst I had put myself through seemed to have been allayed by the easy way we related to each other. Now I am ready for some real connecting - I have made space for that in my heart but where is he - nowhere to be found - nowhere man…

When I woke up, I had a thought about how we need to nurture the relationships in our lives – people say I have green fingers but it's purely because I take care of my plants. You need to plant seeds in good soil, water them, place them in an environment where they will thrive – a healthy balance of sunshine and moisture - and if you do this, a miracle unfolds before your eyes - so I decide to type up something to this effect and send it.

It's Easter time - a time symbolising new life and potential. Am I now clutching at straws? (I never knew exactly where this saying came from – I looked it up and this is what it said – *'The idiom originated with Thomas More's Dialogue of Comfort Against Tribulation (1534). It indicates desperation. A drowning man will clutch/grab at anything, even at straw, in an attempt to save himself'.*

I had chosen the perfect analogy – I felt like I was drowning and whatever I was clutching on to, was not going to save me. I had no idea why this man was backing off and I asked myself, *'Should I really be messaging him?'* Sending him a message is equivalent to thinking a bunch of straw is going to hold my weight and rescue me. I am aware it smacks of desperation but I press send anyway. It's a long shot but there is a small chance he'll realise that this plant needs some loving…

*'I woke up this morning with this thought in my head…every new encounter holds within it the seed of possibility. What it will grow into depends on how we water and nurture it. I thought that was appropriate for this time…Easter…new life! Are u okay?'*

He replies that it's so true and that he's enjoying the long weekend at home…some work, housekeeping, rest and reading. I tell him I'm going to spend the day with the family again tomorrow because my daughter-in-law's mother is here from Australia – he says *'enjoy'*.

Something just doesn't feel right. We went from being in rapport to replies that feel a bit strained. I have no idea what happened. I feel confused. Did I really make all of it up in my mind? This man is just not behaving like he is at all that interested – what changed?

*Like a wild natured cat, your love for him and all the care you put into feeding him and making him comfortable, will never be enough of a hook to reel in this man for keeps. No matter what you offer him, if he feels in any way entrapped by you, you will not be enough for him to come and curl up next to you for long periods of time. He values his time alone more than anything you can offer him – and will fit you into his schedule when it suits him – he will come to you on his own terms. This is realistically what you can expect from him. I know it's not much to go on but now you know, you can make an informed choice.*

## 27ᵗʰ March – Easter Sunday

I am feeling so incredibly down today. Meeting this amazing man brought with it the potential for a different life, filled with new possibilities – I was on the precipice of imagining how nice and cosy it would be to have some intimacy, sex, a companion, somebody to do stuff with, somebody who has my back, who I can trust with my life. Every time I have met a man over the last, I don't know how many years (and that has been seldom), it has ended up being a complete waste of my mental and emotional energy – why did I think this could be any different? It reminds me of the game, Monopoly, where one throw of the dice can send you back to the starting line except that this is my real life and no fun at all.

I never feel so dissatisfied with being alone, as I do after these brief encounters that go absolutely nowhere. I understand that the hopes and dreams I have built around this man are my own projection but it still feels like a slap across the face or a boot kick up my egos ass.  Sub-consciously, I probably don't think I deserve to have something amazing in my life – *"Who the fuck was I to think I can have that? - Why is the universe messing with me - playing some type of warped, sick joke? – Is it really better to have loved and lost than not to have loved at all? That's debatable - surely not? I don't need this shit in my life. I was maintaining and handling my aloneness – just. I didn't need to be tempted by a shiny apple at the top of that big old tree – so near yet so far out of reach – and guess what – on closer inspection it's probably being eaten by worms – inedible and rotten in its core!"*

## 28ᵗʰ March – Easter Monday

…all I write in my diary today is "Who is Enes to me?" I ask this question with clear intent. Enes said if you have a question, in your mind, you must ask it and wait two weeks for your answer. I write down the dates - March 28ᵗʰ to April 11ᵗʰ and then I completely forget about it.

### 29ᵗʰ March – Tuesday

I got a message from Enes - how did the family lunch go? I had to smile. I just don't know with this man. Perhaps we are mirrors - I think he's pulling back and he thinks I'm pulling back. I was so tempted to invite him to the lunch but then he could have seen me on Monday. I wissshhh he would *DO SOMETHING*. I was so excited in every part of my being, to hear from him. I sent a friendly reply back - no response.

> ***If a woman in love with an emotionally unavailable man accepts and gets excited about bread crumbs when in reality she wants a whole loaf then she needs to take a long look at what she thinks she deserves. I understand perfectly that with these men, the smallest sign that they care, can feel like progress because they are generally so elusive. The question is 'Where is your boundary?' If you don't ask for more, then you won't get more and if you ask for more and you are refused then you will at least know where you stand. It's then up to you whether or not you really want to stick around for some, occasionally scattered around you, bread crumbs – just enough to give you something to peck at.***

### April

### 2ⁿᵈ April - Saturday

I'm feeling pretty neutral and numb about Enes. He messaged to say he had a lazy day, hanging around the house, reading, resting and watching movies. He said that he probably just needed to recover that way after being really busy at work. I guess I have no idea about the pressures he experiences at work but as my dear, gay friend says, *'People can make the time to see you if they really want to'*- so he's had a lovely day of rest - what about tomorrow? I didn't say that. I just felt let down by my own expectations of how I thought it would evolve, according to my own perception of what I wanted. He had never let on – never even insinuated that he felt the same about me.

*Don't expect to have a tomorrow with an emotionally unavailable man. He is volatile and does not know exactly where he will be tomorrow. The only thing that you can consistently rely on, is inconsistency. And you will never know if he misses you in your absence or what he is feeling – that's what makes him emotionally unavailable, remember – he is probably not experiencing any. If he is sticking around, in a manner of speaking, all you will know is that there is something about the contact with you that he enjoys but what that something is, could forever remain a complete enigma.*

I had an awful, soul destroying experience at the shops today. A woman approached me saying that she has a twelve year old son and they are starving - could I help with some cash. My heart went out to her – she seemed so real. I'm usually pretty good at picking up a con but when in doubt, I reckon it's better to help than just leave somebody destitute. I decided to buy her some food instead of money and told her so. That way I would make sure that her child actually got fed. I went into the store and did a grocery shop with easy to prepare meals in mind. When I got out, she was nowhere to be found. She clearly didn't need food. Fortunately the store offered me a refund because I don't eat things like pasta anymore. I really felt distraught about it. I guess I am questioning, 'Where is the integrity, in the world', and sadly that goes for the people in my life too. It upset me terribly because it's indicative of more severe, underlying issues in our lifestyle and our society today.

When I got home, I replied to Enes's earlier message with a long message about how I had nearly been taken in by a con. I just needed to vent to someone in hope that somebody out there actually gives a damn – especially him.

### 3ʳᵈ April - Sunday

I didn't get a reply to my message last night. On the one hand he sends encouraging messages saying how much he loves the little emoticons I always include – they make him smile – the next he just ignores me. I am beginning to doubt my own common sense and I am beginning to feel bipolar in my inner being – I am so up and down with this – the only thing I am sure about, is what I feel for this man.

*If you are looking to this man to emotionally secure you then you have come to the wrong place. Unless you have your own emotional maps and resources, to guide you through this unpredictability, you may begin to doubt yourself – are you emotionally messed up - are you imagining things that aren't there? – did he or did he not show signs of being into you – If I'm that unstable how will I ever be able to have any semblance of a normal love life ever again?*

*(My friend, Kendall, who had known Enes a long time, reassured me that it wasn't anything I was doing or not doing. He was the one who was paranoid about relationships and intimacy, not me – I then realised that the only way this intelligent man would sort out his issues, was if he decided he wanted to do it for himself. He was never going to do it for me – perhaps if he came to genuinely love me, he would make that decision but we were nowhere near that and possibly never would be...we were still at this very drawn out 'checking it out stage'...at least that's what I told myself).*

I try not to indulge in victim thoughts about how it never works with men. I convince myself that I haven't invested enough yet for a major amount of damage control if he leaves but then I correct myself - how can he leave when he was never here at all - not really?

Later, I receive a message to say that he has sent an email because his reply was too long to type in a message - I have to smile a big inner smile - he cared enough to send an email response. What the f*#k is wrong with me? Why am I so insecure?

He had invested a lot of time, writing me a long email, some of it about the experience I had and how convincing some of these con artists are and also about some issues I had mentioned that I have with my in-laws in a previous message – he spoke about how we tend to bring emotion into situations with noncore people in our lives by attaching words such as connection, trust, valuable or loving to the relationship. He said that this creates an expectation from our side and people may not always respond the way we would like so it's better to remain neutral without judgment. He said it feels more empowering as it doesn't create a link to that person and he often speaks to his team at work about this but it is quite a tricky topic.

I didn't get the impression that he was being pointed about anything to do with us specifically, but some clues were beginning to unravel about how this emotionally unavailable man thinks. I wondered if there was a *warning* in his email. There seems to be a big movement, at the moment, about how to avoid, what people are calling, our *negative emotions*. It's largely male driven and I have to admit, what he had said, began toying with my mind. I don't agree that all emotions that create discomfort are *negative*. When somebody dies or we go through a break up and lose somebody we love, it is natural to grieve and experience pain – so where exactly is the line between healthy negative emotions and unhealthy ones? I have always believed that my emotions are my guidance system and I definitely don't want to disassociate from them in order to protect myself from *feeling – good or bad*.

His email showed that he cared enough about me to spend time being thoughtful and I chose to see the positive in that. He ended off saying that he was doing research and studying for a new product they were launching. Once again, he had taken time to engage with me on a deeper level, between his work commitments. I made a mental note that at some point, I would have a proper discussion with him about emotions and how I view them but not today, in an email – that would have to wait for a *maybe* face to face in the *maybe* future we had.

I admire the fact that Enes has explored the inner workings of the mind and is sharing his insights with me - it indicates that he actually does have emotional intelligence, although, perhaps, leaning towards being a bit extreme but I do really enjoy this about him - it's a big part of what attracts me to him - the reason why he is so different from other men I have met over the years yet it strikes me that what he is expressing is completely impersonal – he could be writing to anybody. Is this what he is doing with me, a non-core person in his life - remaining neutral?

'*The important thing,*' I tell myself, '*is that he cared enough to take the time to email me*' and I also sense that this man can teach me something for a change. It's refreshing and is a big stepping out from my usual pattern - a man who can actually teach me something. There have been so few of those, if any? A question my father asked me, springs to mind, "*Lilith, why do you always undersell yourself with men?*" – If - and it's a big *IF* there is any future with this man, I would tell my father, '*Not this time Daddy, you would like him!*"

**Emotionally unavailable men can be emotionally intelligent. I know this sounds like a complete contradiction. Most men will not delve deeper into their feelings to try and understand them – they would rather drown their sorrows in distractions like binge drinking with their mates or screwing around. This type of man may know he is emotionally unavailable but he will have no clue as to why. An emotionally intelligent, unavailable man has more insight than most - about how emotions impact on our outer and inner worlds. They have simply and knowingly removed their own**

*hearts from the equation and chosen to view emotions purely intellectually, as a topic – more like subject matter to explore.*

As I sit and contemplate Enes's writing, I have the sensation, yet again, of expanding. His email didn't give me any reason to draw closer to him but my heart knows what it wants and it is opening up to him – and through this opening, I am beginning to sense stirrings that I am also opening up to life again. In this moment, I experience an energetic connection to him I can't explain – there is no basis for it from the outside looking in. I know that things are not always as they seem, on the surface and that an energetic connection can be as real as a physical connection - I decide not to analyse it too much. These moments have become so few and far between in my life so I allow it. I give myself permission - to feel it!

In my book, The Other Side of My Reflection I wrote about a room with no view :-

*"The rest of the afternoon passed by, in a hazy awareness of distant emotions that sat silently in some part of my body, where I had stored all the other pain. It was like a room with no view or door, no window to look out from. Somehow it absorbed the pain into its walls by osmosis and there the feelings sat like trapped little prisoners on death row, in no man's land, experiencing neither life nor death, nor release. The room was lost, floating somewhere in the cells of my body and I was lost to the room."* – The Other Side of My Reflection – Lilith White

I have this thought - *'Today I flung that door wide open'.*

I respond to what he has shared and then I decide to venture into new territory - *the room with no view* - and my fear of men. I am now treading into uncharted territory with this man. Here I am about to take a risk. So far I have given him the impression that I am content to be single. Now I tell him that the deeper part of me would love to have a partner, lover, soul mate, best friend and that my natural inclination is not to live without touch and companionship - it's just been easier and less risky not to go there. I have a lot of fear about men. I did not say that I wanted that specifically with him but I guess that must have been pretty obvious.

I know that most men don't like it when a woman opens up this window. It was a big risk - it could be what my dad had said to me once — *"Next time you meet a man, don't fuck it up"* - but if this man is thinking of going there with me, there are things he needs to know about me - well, that's what I tell myself - or could this just be the beginning of self sabotage - pushing boundaries to test him? I don't fully understand what my unconscious reasons are for doing this. He could run - if he was going to run, now would be the time - but he didn't. He replied that he would answer during the week and he confirmed this with a cell message to make sure I got it. He wasn't running but clearly needed to chew on it for a while...

## 4th April - Monday

My Turkish Tomato seeds are shooting. When Enes visited me with the organic veg, I immediately took the tomato seeds outside and quickly dug them into a plant pot - yes in between all the cooking - I know, crazy but hey, my green fingers didn't want to lose the opportunity of having them in my garden and there is no time like the present moment, right? There are three tiny shoots pushing and stretching themselves out of the soil and I am beside myself excited about it. I took a photo and sent it to Enes saying *'Every time a seed shoots it's like watching a little miracle in action'*. He replied immediately, *'It confirms the progression of life'* I don't think he's running - not just yet - waiting for that email then we shall see????

## 6th April - Wednesday

Enes sent me a message saying he has sent an email — this one is a biggie — I wonder how exactly he will respond to me saying that I would love to have intimacy in my life. I am so nervous to open and read it but here goes...

His email reply is long and well thought out. I can tell he has had disappointments in his life – he talks about learning to disassociate to keep a healthy equilibrium without over-judging, over-compensating, over-giving, over-compromising ourselves. He mentions that I have raised two well balanced children and I should be very proud of myself. He says that once I get all these balances right in my life, all will be well - that's the gist of it. It had been an opening for him to give me some indication of how he feels about me but there was nothing to suggest that he feels anything for me, on a personal level, besides the fact that he has taken so long to reply and took the time to write a long email - perhaps that was more than most men would have done in this, perhaps uncomfortable, situation.

*An emotionally unavailable man will find it extremely difficult to define what your relationship means to him – he may even have a problem with the word relationship. You will have to make peace with this if you want him in your life. You are not going to change him and any demands to do so will have him scampering in the opposite direction, further away from you. You may find out that although he is generally a nice guy, he can become very cold and almost cruel when he is defending his unavailable position. I'm not advocating that you don't express or take your own needs into account. You are perfectly entitled to be upfront about it. This is just to let you know what you can or can't expect if you decide you have the patience to stick around. If your bottom line is that you want all or nothing, best you go seeking elsewhere. There are lots more lovable cats out there, just waiting for you to take them in.*

## 7th April - Thursday

I sent Enes a very long reply to his email, sharing my thoughts about a myriad of scenarios – I had spent a large part of my life, giving to people altruistically and believing that unconditional love could conquer all – I had reached a point, where it had become clear that sometimes people have to work for it and reciprocate to earn that place in my life – it was now not a given. I had been hurt and disappointed along the way, so in certain aspects of the conversation, I was in total agreement with him. I concluded that I don't often extend myself and invite men into my space nowadays. I wanted him to know that he was unique and special - it was not something I did often.

This began our more regular, almost daily, email sharing - however, he was never personal about *us* and never even hinted that he was attracted to me in any way other than somebody he enjoyed bouncing ideas off.

*There is a reason why your crush is emotionally unavailable. Of course I didn't know any of this yet – will he face any of your openness head on and give you the same back in return. No silly, he is emo-tion-ally UNAVAILABLE. He is a good guy so he kept his word about sending a reply later in the week – was he going to go there....NOOOO...he was going to tackle it in his unavailable type of way – generally, not personally. I'm not saying that just because he can't go there means that you shouldn't go there. I have always tried to be authentic in my relationships with people – anything other than that becomes a type of game playing – some women are good at this and get better results than I do.*

*We are advised to be mysterious and to keep our hearts close to our chests. Good or bad, I am the extreme opposite of this. I am upfront and people know exactly where they stand with me. There is nothing wrong with being more elusive about yourself – I am not advocating pouring your heart out, but there will come a time when it becomes important to face and state clearly what it is you really want. Either this or you can continue for a time or even years to have this same relationship with this person you would like to have more with – painful isn't it?*

## 8th April – Friday

Enes and I are covering a lot of ground. We've been emailing each other backwards and forwards the last couple days and sending lots of cell messages in between. It's like this man is so much a part of my life but in reality, he is still only a long distance pen pal. I have a 30th birthday party tomorrow night – my daughter-in-law's brother - and I am wondering if I could invite him. Usually a party like this would be the perfect excuse to invite a potential mate but I honestly don't think he will enjoy it. I doubt whether I will enjoy it. I am going because Katz's brother and his wife really like me a lot. We get on well and I think I need to show my face. If I thought he would feel comfortable there, I would invite him but I still feel we haven't spent enough one on one time together. Besides, it's another weekend and another opportunity for him to make a plan to see me and he hasn't made any moves or suggestions in that direction…

## 9th April – Saturday

I get dressed for the 30th reluctantly. I am so tired of showing up at these parties single. I have known all these people for years and they have never seen me with a man, but once again it's not appropriate to invite my 'ish' crush to a family gathering of people who are not really even my immediate family.

I go to the party – it's six months since I had Pancreatitis and I am now allowed to do alcohol. I decide to drink a couple beers.

Maybe it will lighten me up and I'll be able to have some silly fun. The beers just loosen my tongue and make me more verbally honest than is good for me – saying some things I should probably not have said at all - and everybody seems to be having conversations that I can't even begin to relate to. I am changed and I am bored. I stay for food and the lighting of the candles.

I decide to leave early. There is only one thing I really want in my life right now – the Turk with the expansive mind – the man I am crushing on all by myself – but he is absent – these are private thoughts and spaces. I imagine how snuggling up next to him to watch a movie would be much more exciting than the emptiness I feel at this party. Yeah, only in my dreams, right – and would the reality be half as enthralling as I have envisioned in the *movie in my mind* – that remains to be seen – or not seen. I'm happy to leave and go home, either way.

## April 10ᵗʰ – Sunday

Today was a bit bizarre - all this messaging and emailing doesn't seem to be getting us any closer to a real connection. I awake feeling a certain amount of neutrality about the situation - the calm before the storm, I guess. I decide to go online to see when last he was active and seconds later a message comes through asking how my weekend is going? He has sent an email.

I was excited - another email. I was looking forward to it. I opened it up with bated breath. He is talking about toxic relationships and if something about a connection disturbs you, it should be a sign not to go there. My initial reaction is '*he's dumping me - he's fucking dumping me!*' Not that he was ever really there. A strange calm washes over me. I think a part of me felt a small tinge of relief - now I can just run back into my comfort zone – insular and reclusive. I write a reply from this perspective then I read his message again and realise that I may have misconstrued what he was saying - then I doubt myself - maybe I didn't misread it – then maybe I did – I'm perplexed. I decide to go with my initial gut reaction – maybe it's for the best. I press send then I send him a text saying that it's okay... I understand where he's coming from.

It doesn't take long for a reply to come through.

*'I wasn't' talking about you'* then he sends another email and tells me that he resonates with me – it is the *very first time* he has alluded to the fact that he really likes me  - can this be called progress - dare I trust the booming of my heart in this moment ?

I then realise that he may actually have been planning to see me today but now I have made it all very awkward. Do I ask him to come over? I want to see him but I surprise myself with the realisation that as much as I've been longing to see him, I am now observing resistance in myself, *'I am scared and it's almost easier not to know - not knowing how this story ends keeps me cocooned in illusion - I want to feel safe for a little while longer'.*  I had been so intent on attributing the lack of face to face contact to his unavailability that I had never even considered that keeping each other at a comfortable distance had been partly my own doing. Once again, it struck me that I am his mirror? Is there a part of me that has also become emotionally unavailable?

## Later

I send him a message and wish him a nice long sleep because I know how broken his sleep patterns are and tell him that I'm just about to watch a Sean Penn movie. My phone beeps and I have a reply from both him and a message from Jay (the guy I connected with on the long weekend away – he has also been messaging me ever since). I'm not really sure what I want to do about Jay – but I can't even go there right now – from nothing to two men at the same time - what the F**k? I am beside myself excited about Enes's message – I do my *waiting thing* before I open it - I sense it could be something big - Enes wants to see me tomorrow - this is very far from a man dumping me - sounds more like a man wanting to secure me. I reply that would be great. I have no idea what to say to Jay. I really like him a lot - but not in that way - and I'm trying to focus on a movie - but the dialogue has become strangely incoherent and I have completely lost the plot. My emotions are somersaulting - I'm flying on an energetic high on top of that Ferris Wheel - and I'm completely distracted - *'I am going to see Enes tomorrow - I'm going to see Enes tomorrow'* - I'm trying to stay grounded - not completely lose my balance, but my heart is expanding out of my chest and I can't think straight. I can't contain my excitement. I message Jay to be polite and tell him I'm watching a movie - and wonder if I should just be honest with him.

I go to bed to write in my journal. The book falls open on the page that says March 28th to April 11th. Tomorrow it will be two weeks, to the day, since I asked *'Who is Enes to me?'* It's astoundingly co-incidental, if there is such a thing as co-incidence. Tomorrow it will be exactly two weeks and I will finally have the olive skinned Turk's, solid presence, in my home again. I cannot help but find the synchronicity mind blowing - and who visits on a Monday anyway? I try not to make too much of a big deal out of it - we shall see what answer tomorrow brings.

## 11ᵗʰ April - Monday

Today Enes will come for dinner. I decide to let Jay know that I'm not in the market for a relationship. I want to give the universe clear signals right now. Enes is the man I want in my life. Jay comes back to me telling me that he finds me sexy - that he seldom pursues women but wants to pursue something with me. He says he felt it from the moment he saw me. I have to confess that my ego really laps up this stroking. I haven't had any attention from men for so long and now this guy is affirming that I am attractive and desirable - who knew? For the longest time I've believed I'd lost all traces of being desired by men. In that moment I feel immense gratitude for Jay. Enes has been so elusive and now Jay is reassuring me - empowering me to believe in myself through this *still checking it out* stage with the Turk. Knowing I have another man who is crazy about me, even though I do not feel the same, is helping me to maintain some semblance of balance as I prepare for this *not so new man anymore, tightrope act.* I pray I will not come crashing down – I will see Enes tomorrow.

I spend the day tidying, cleaning and shifting my space. I am clearing out my emotional house to let Enes into my life. I observe some resistance I have during the day. It is so much easier to just be alone. I don't have to challenge myself or do or be anything for anybody else - but I want love in my life and he is the *only* man I have felt this about since, what feels like, forever.

At three-ish I get a message to say he is leaving work at 4:30 and coming straight over, if that's okay? I am ready for this - I AM READY! I shower then roll the pre-soaked falafel mix into little patties and fry them so I don't have to spend so much of our precious time together, standing over the stove like last time - I titivate. I know that's a weird, antiquated word but I read it in a Home Economics Text Book when I was in school. The syllabus clearly needed updating, even then. It said that a woman should prepare the house and dinner before her husband gets home and then *'titivate'* - at the time I found this extremely hilarious…*'titivate before your hard working husband comes home'* - how woman were conditioned in those days - so I use the word, completely tongue in cheek.

I stack logs next to the fire burner in the sitting room - throw a beautiful, funky cloth over the garden table - arrange cushions on the bench that overlooks the expansive garden and I affirm again - I AM READY!

He arrives. I go up to meet him at the car. We give each other one of those noncommittal hugs, hello. He says he has brought some goodies. I don't know why but flowers cross my mind - there are no flowers. I wonder if he had thought about flowers and then changed his mind. Sometimes I just know these things but guess I will never know. He brought melon, bean salad and some fruit juice - the real thing, he tells me, not one made from concentrate. I look at his face. He is like a stranger. I had almost forgotten what he looks like yet it is easy and there is a sense of familiarity between us, a simpatico that I guess, boils down to all that messaging and all those lengthy emails. We do already know one another quite well. I tell him I am grateful for the salad because the thought had crossed my mind that I needed one to go with the meal. He tells me he walked straight to it, insinuating that he had picked it up - like he had read my mind.

Enes builds a fire while I prepare the meal. I want to photograph him there with the flames leaping up behind him but I don't. I had been threatening to make a fire, with the evenings getting cooler but this was the first one I had actually had. It warmed the house beautifully. I had set my little dining table for two. Last time we had eaten on the coffee table and I wanted it to be more comfortable, more engaging. We had a lot to share - we spoke about him arriving in South Africa the same year my husband died. He told me about his brother who gets under his skin. He is apparently slow - mentally challenged. I thought about how my own brother always manages to get under my skin, and always wonder what that is about. We both had to endure fathers who were extremely slow eaters and sit at the table watching them eat. I know this sounds a bit like those movie moments when boy meets girl and they just love all the same things - well, it was kind of like that - we felt connected like the universe had been lining us up to meet at this particular time and had been preparing our meeting for many years. When he told me he'd arrived in South Africa the year my husband died I said, '*That is weird*' but in actual fact it's not really weird but it struck me as quite profound in that moment.  He warned me that my friend, Dona, isn't cool - so he had picked up how she had been subtly or not so subtly flirting with him.

It was another successful dinner - just the two of us. There were no overtures or romantic gestures. He did not try to touch me and our goodbye hug was, again, as noncommittal as all the previous ones but this man definitely did not feel like *only a friend* - it still felt very much like we were checking it out, even though two snails would have been moving faster. There is something different about just friends. He feels more like a boyfriend even though there has been nothing physical between us…why?

*What it is and why are always the big questions surrounding a relationship with an emotionally avoidant man. It will always be difficult to pin point exactly what it is – he may seem to be doing most of the things that a boyfriend would do and your time together may always be time well spent and it appears to be mutual – all the same, you need to bear in mind that he is not your boyfriend and perhaps never will be.*

> *Enjoy your time together but don't expect him back any time soon – in fact, don't expect anything. If you want this man in your life, you have to be in constant readiness to always let him go. If you can let him go enough to live happily on your own, with no promises of when you will meet again, after every time he says goodbye then you will be an emotionally unavailable man's perfect woman/friend/acquaintance or whatever cap fits the connection, in the moment.*

## 12ᵗʰ April - Tuesday

I woke up this morning, to an inner world that had been completely rearranged. I couldn't fall asleep until around 3:30. My mind had been buzzing with thoughts about Enes. After he left, last night, I went to the bathroom. I looked in the mirror and couldn't contain my elation, *'I think I have a boyfriend – I really think I have a boyfriend'* I had told my reflection convincingly - I did a crazy little jig. There are so many parallels with Enes that seem to imply a deeper connection than what I could even have imagined. I do believe, wholeheartedly, in reincarnation and that shared past lifetimes together were more than likely. Spending time with him again had confirmed why I had fallen for him and I was reassured that I wasn't completely delusional - but then I think I had already fallen for him, pretty much at, *'Hello are you Turkish?'*

I no longer believe it's only one sided – he had come to secure me - he was definitely in my life and far from stepping out – he had warned me about Dona, which was a clever way of telling me he's not into her.

I am now hovering between certainty and doubt – he didn't give me any obvious signs that he is anything more than a friend to me and I don't fully understand what any of this really means - from me asking on the 28ᵗʰ to him coming over exactly two weeks later but does that actually answer my question, *'Who is Enes to me?'* I don't trust myself enough to read these signs accurately - healthy scepticism will shield me from disappointment - I don't want to set myself up for pain by placing any agenda on to this - at the same time, it all feels so extremely synchronistic and meant to be, which makes it very difficult not to place an expectation on to it - I have to be careful of not projecting more on to it than what I have right here, right now, in front of me - but after last night I am convinced that we are mirroring each other. Has my question been answered - I realise that I still have no idea who Enes is to me...

I would love to be able to encapsulate the essence of the night with him and capture it here on paper but sometimes our inner worlds are beyond words. How do we even talk about these things? There are very few times in my life where I am lost for words but I am unable to describe my connection with this person - it feels unknowable. I have a feeling that if Enes and I were in each other's company and we didn't say one word to each other, there would still be an understanding between us - a telepathy of minds that already knows before anything is expressed...

The question now is - does he feel this too? And if so, is he going to take a few steps closer?

## 12ᵗʰ April – Tuesday

Enes messaged me to say thanks for the great time and nice food and that he had had a great, long sleep and only woke up at six. For a man who suffers from insomnia this speaks volumes. He obviously felt balanced and content after being with me. It really warmed my heart, knowing that through our contact, Enes was able to relax and sleep soundly. We sent a couple messages backwards and forwards.

Later, just before his bedtime, I felt comfortable enough to express some things around our connection - that people seldom 'get me' and I thanked him for *seeing me*. He said that our souls can relate to each other and that we catch a common frequency (I find how he expresses things in his Turkish way so appealing). This was pretty much the most personal thing he had ever said to me and it felt like a leap into new territory. I was lulled into a false sense of security as a comfortable sense of peace washed over me - perhaps now we could relax into the next phase of our connection. The new relationship angst had dissipated and I looked forward to the future prospects of having this solid, grounding force of a man, actively in my life.

## 13th April – Wednesday

Today I closed the door on an old friendship. My friend, Lisa, is without a car and I have my daughter's car just standing here. I offered it to her, after fixing the starter motor and she said she would ask her cousin, who she is staying with, to bring her to collect it. We didn't arrange an exact time. I needed something from the shops, down the road, so I decided to quickly pop down. It is just around the corner and if Lisa was on her way, I could get home quickly before they arrived. When I got to the shops I messaged her to say I was at the shops, just in case she arrived and I wouldn't be long. She knows how close the local store is to me so there couldn't have been any misunderstanding. The next minute my phone rings. It's Lisa. I pick up, *'Hello'* - silence - then I hear her talking to her cousin and *I can hear everything*! She is complaining about me going to the shops NOW and why did I have to go to the shops when I knew she was on her way and whatever else she was saying about me became a blur in my mind - a rampage of criticisms and judgements. It sounded like she had no respect for me or even liked me. I was stunned!

I kept saying, *"Lisa…LISA…I CAN HEAR EVERYTHING YOU ARE SAYING ABOUT ME!!!!"* The most astounding thing is that she made it sound like she was coming over to do me a favour - not the other way round. I was giving her a car for *fucks sake*. It was a kick in the teeth and I was extremely angry. I messaged her to say she had *'pocked dialled'* me and I had heard everything she said about me and the car deal was off. She replied that she had not pocket dialled me - her phone was in her bag. *'Daaah, pocket dialled is not literal,'* I felt like screaming into the phone but I didn't grace her with a response - that was it - a friendship just died a shitty death!

Enes seems to be becoming more valuable and relevant to me as my other friendships fall away. I think of it as a type of cleansing - the old toxic relationships are leaving my life, of their own accord, and I am replacing them with awesome people like Enes. I then remind myself that I don't *actually* know what people like Enes are *really* like - I still know very little about him. I sense he has integrity - I want to believe he is there for me. A little warning bell goes off in my head - what were his words - don't ascribe words like *valuable* and *relevant* to noncore people in your life. He never insinuated that he was or would ever be a core person in my life - only time can reveal this and it was too soon to tell...I had to wait and see.

## 15ᵗʰ April – Friday

I wrote in my journal – '*I LOVE THE UNIVERSE*'

I wake up in a bad space. The aftermath of our dinner date has been an anti-climax - this man is showing no signs of continuity - sure, we message each other pretty much *ALL THE TIME*. It feels like we are so connected yet going absolutely nowhere at the same time. I tell myself to be patient but I want to know! Am I building castles in the sand again? I am incapacitated from doing pretty much anything. My heart is all tangled up for Enes - I've got it so bad for him...

I decide to do some gardening to ground myself and focus on something I love doing – mother earth, soil and plants are my soul food. My son sends me the cutest pictures of each one of the boys inside a bucket with their little heads sticking out. They are such adorable photos and I realise that I really do want to have somebody, permanently in my life to share my special moments with - like this one. I forwarded them to Enes to make him smile. He replies that they are such cute kids and it must make me feel all warm inside - I don't tell him how warm he made me feel, inside and out, when he was building that fire to heat up my home

He tells me the team are on high alert for a new product launch tomorrow night and that he won't be able to rest until Sunday when he knows it was a success. I message back to express that the energies have been very positive this week and

I'm sending him good vibes - one minute that's what I'm feeling then I start going downhill. What the hell am I doing - what exactly am I doing falling for this man? I had told him, initially, that I didn't have the resources for a relationship - he had agreed on friendship - but then he had come to secure me after I had confessed that I really did want love and intimacy in my life - and every time I see him I fall more deeply for him.

I'm building castles in the sand - and we all know what happens to those - they melt into the sea, eventually. There is no real foundation for me to believe in what I would like to happen next or for a future with him. There is a saying, *'The heart wants what the heart wants'*. It's like the tide that destroys the castles. It is unstoppable. How do you put a lid on falling in love - screw it shut and bottle it up like a preserve that looks so pretty on the shelf that you never get to taste it.

The weekend looms in front of me. I don't even have Lisa to escape to anymore. I had received an email invitation from Dona, earlier in the week, to a farewell party she was having before moving house. Perhaps I could push my feelings about her aside and go to that - but do I want to encourage a friendship with a woman who has no integrity with her women friends?

So I started today's page with *I LOVE THE UNIVERSE* - here's why; A message comes in from Dona - am I coming? I message back that I haven't decided yet. A thought goes through my mind that she is going to tell me to invite Enes because that's actually what the invitation is really all about - I doubt myself and think I'm just being malicious but within minutes, my prediction materialises in the form of a text, *'You can invite Enes if you want?'*

*'Oh, my gosh, this woman is so transparent.'* I'm not an aggressive person, but I feel like smacking those words right out of her mouth.

Normally Enes is completely unavailable to me on weekends and I have no idea where he goes or what he does - mostly it sounds like he stays at home and watches movies or does overtime for work but I honestly don't really know exactly - but it just so happens that I know *exactly* what he is doing tomorrow night. He never lets me know about his weekend plans but today he did. In that moment, I love the universe so very, very much - I don't even have to wrack my brain to find some excuse. I can stay in complete integrity from my side - I reply, *'Enes has a product launch tomorrow night so won't be able to make it. Thanks'*. She doesn't reply - not even, well, I hope to see you - and this is a person I called *friend* for the last fifteen years up until a month or two ago. She obviously thinks I'm obtuse like I have no inkling about her intensions to ensnare the man of *my* dreams - nice friend. First Lisa, now this - two of my oldest friends.

I was so delighted I was able to give the impression that Enes and I are enmeshed in each other's lives - that I know exactly what he will be doing and when. My friend Clinty says it's my time now and I affirm this with a big 'yessss' to that. I bless the universe, one more time, for the perfect synchronicity - there is now no possibility that I can wear a fake mask, as an excuse to leave the house and go to her party. I would prefer never to lay eyes on her again. I will just have to find a way to embrace my aloneness – find peace with my isolation and self reflection.

## *Later*

This evening I feel like I've run into a brick wall face first and came back down to earth with a big bang. I'm feeling so extremely dented, emotional and down on the human race. What the f*#K is going on? Two friends have shown their true colours, in a matter of days. I long for a solid shoulder to lean on – somebody who will never desert me. Coming home from ICU had been a huge eye opener for me. I had to face the lack of support, in my life, square on. Besides my son, who popped in every day to make sure I had food (I was too weak to make food or even dish up food), none of my so-called friends, had been around. Now I had to face the fact that I didn't even have the *illusion* of a remote support system and Enes hasn't been around enough, for me to know for sure, whether he is in or out.

He didn't reply to my *up* message about the good energies and I was sending him positive vibes across the cell waves - and now that just feels like a load of bullshit – the energies are crap right now. I completely get that he is extremely busy and he warned me about it. I know I'm being a baby - emotionally messed up, hurting and my self esteem is damaged - I still have nothing to go on - no promise of a future something and I'm falling - falling -

falling head over heels in love and it scares the *heebie-geebies* out of me...

I remind myself again what I had told Enes, in the beginning about not having the emotional resources for relationships. New love relationships require stamina, attention, inner strength and courage, which I don't have at the moment. It's a catch 22. I want something I am clearly not emotionally equipped to have - the only way this could have worked is if it started out as a friendship and if he was crazy about me like Jay is crazy about me - and this is clearly not the case. I said I didn't want a romantic relationship - we agreed. That was my doing. I instigated the pact between us. It was my inner truth at the time. It wasn't a lie. Now I've fallen for him -  I want more but at the same time I feel too broken to do this. *'I know where this road ends and I can't do it again, ever!'* It is so much easier not feeling anything for anybody. Why did I have to arrive on this earth as a highly sensitive person - an intensely emotional being? Maybe I can take his advice and learn the art of disassociation...

Nighty night diary. Tomorrow is another day - I still wait in anticipation for what will happen next...

## 16ᵗʰ April - Sunday

Today I wake up with a resolve to channel my energy into my next book, The Men-o-pause Diaries. I start sorting through my old diaries and begin reading a 2011 journal and it is so gloomy that I could dig a hole and bury myself in it right here on the spot. I can't face writing this book now. It was such a difficult time in my life - there was far too much pain. Through everything I ever went through, I had never had thoughts about wishing to die but today a thought crosses my mind that I should have died in that ICU - without medical intervention I would be dead - perhaps that had been my destined, soul journey and I had messed with the natural order. It would have been easier to give up, curl up and die - to be released from all the pain and future hurts that I feel I need to consistently prepare for, just in case...

Even if Enes finally reciprocates my feelings for him, there are no guarantees it will not end in pain. That is just the nature of taking a chance in relationships - there are no guarantees so the question comes up again, *'Is it really better to have loved and lost than not to have loved at all - is it really better?'* Better in what way - you opened your heart - you made yourself vulnerable enough to let love in then you got a boot kick up the arse - how is that better? How is this dark place I find myself in, because I have fallen for a man who doesn't feel the same, better than not having met him at all? Why did I even go to that farewell at Kendall - I wasn't going to go. What possessed me? I feel like I'm drowning - always drowning - I allowed myself to feel something for this man and I have completely lost my balance - I'm struggling to function and Lisa and Dona are a big, fat, rotten cherry on top of this stale cake.  It's too much. I am supposed to be healing. I get that it's probably healthy to close the door on my toxic relationships with these women but that leaves me floating - marooned on an island - a desert in suburbia where there are hundreds of strangers out there that I do not know and who don't know me. How is it possible that I ended up so secluded?

My daughter says I must rather be alone than invest energy in takers. She says Dona is an energy vamp and always has been – *'Just do what you love – your writing and your gardening and be alone!'* My daughter is such a wise woman and I know she is right. I have found contentment, in the past, in that space. I can do it again. I know how to do that.

I also need to take a long, realistic, hard look at how I fall inappropriately for men. I latch on to my own illusions as if they are real - are they really that far removed from reality and if so is there something intrinsically wrong with me? Enes said that his lifestyle and work don't allow space for a relationship. I mirrored his sentiment at the time - then I make up all sorts of stories in my head about how awesome it would be if we went for it. Am I now lying to myself? Perhaps he just knows himself better than I know myself - the truth is that I don't have the resources to do this - it's too hard to fall in love. I don't have the energy to lose my balance and fall off the tightrope. I will land in a mangled heap and only have myself to blame – I should run…

> *Emotionally avoidant men most often attract women who are insecure in relationships. An insecure woman needs loads of re-assurance. The question is why these two complete opposites attract one another? It is a given that if a woman falls in love with an emotionally distant man that her insecurities will be highlighted. As painful as the relationship is that this man puts you through, the blessing is that it is an opportunity to look at your own patterns in relationship and work on your own issues. Invest the time in between seeing each other – and there will be time in between – to work on yourself.*

## 17ᵗʰ *April Sunday*

I wake up in, poor me, *victim mode*. Lately my Sundays revolve around what is absent instead of what I can create - the man I don't have - the friends I don't have - the intimacy I imagined I could have - the one person - and I only need one - who has my back - instead of this emptiness that aches inside of me.

I feel like my heart is being wrung out like a juicy lemon being squeezed to make somebody else's lemonade, and each little pip that gets thrown into the trash are like the lost egg credits, that had been allocated to me when I arrived into this God forsaken world – now a barren, infertile, useless, loveless woman... with no more cards in my hand to play. Would anybody ever love me again?

The high I felt after the dinner with Enes seems to have reached another dead end plateau, with no continuity. I decide to put on loud *feel good music* and access my *sparkly teenager* who dances around the house while she cleans. The exercise is incredibly uplifting. The reality is that I am not a part of Enes's life - who he sees or what he does. I am a woman inside a phone or computer - this seems to be my new, safe pattern with men - a phone buddy or an email pen pal. I am not a living breathing woman to him - tangible with real blood and passion coursing through my veins - a woman with desires, hopes and a future alive with possiblity.

I know what Enes is doing this weekend but generally his behaviour is not typical of a man who's interested. I wonder what he got up to on all the other, missed opportunity, weekends. He has a secretive life. He doesn't seem to want to be seen in public. Is there perhaps another woman or women? What do I really know about him?

I only know what Kendall has told me and she said he has a private life that she knows nothing about, and she's known him for four years - and why only dinners on week nights? We have been sharing lots of detailed, long distance emails when he lives twenty minutes away - why? Is he hiding his relationship with me away from somebody else? I also understand that things are often not as they seem and I can't jump to conclusions. He said he was single when I met him in December but that was over four months ago - is he still actually single? I just assumed he was alone, then I remembered the doggie bags. A man doesn't take food home, cooked by another woman - okay so maybe she doesn't live with him. Maybe they just see each other over weekends. And what about the whole conversation where he said he can't make plans and he prefers *ad lib* getting together - was that really about Adrenal Fatigue? What when he has a gap to get away - or what?

*This is the way it goes with self-professed emotionally unavailable men – you will always be left guessing about what exactly is going on because their behaviour does not follow any relationship norms. They are a law unto themselves. They do not let you in enough to even question them. You will start believing that you are being completely irrational. They haven't exactly given you any reason to believe that they're potentially your boyfriend and you don't feel entitled to ask questions or to even have feelings for them. Everything feels incongruent and out of sync and you don't know why. This guessing game goes hand in hand with falling for an emotionally avoidant man because they do not let you in on any level. You will begin to wonder if there is something intrinsically wrong with you. You were warned - this is not a walk in the park on a sunny day.*

## 18th April – Monday

After days of unnecessary angst and imagining the worst scenarios in order to protect myself from more disappointment, a message finally comes through from Enes. He says they worked through until four in the morning on the launch - it was successful and he is relieved it's over. How am I? Do I reply that I feel like such an idiot for putting myself through so much trauma? The man is dedicated to his job - he is married to his job and that includes his weekends. What don't I understand about this simple information?

A man who doesn't care about you doesn't message you to explain why he had been absent - a man who doesn't care about you just doesn't give a damn. I go from hopelessness to hope and I tell myself I have to work on how I keep sabotaging myself. I am so relieved to hear from Enes.

## 20th April - Wednesday

There is seriously something wrong with me. I am overwhelmed by melancholy, which makes me wonder if any man would ever want to be with somebody like me - even if Enes decided to go for it, would he be able to cope with this aspect of me? Night times bring with them a real darkness. The loneliness and isolation bears down on me like a dense fog. I can't wait until it's late enough to go to bed. I can't focus on watching movies or series. I wish the time away so I can escape into sleep and not have to think.  My future, in general, is very daunting and the non-existent dating situation with Enes, is really getting me down.

The worst part is the lying to myself about my situation or the pretending to him that everything in my world is perfectly *hunky-dory* - like I'm playing a part in some dysfunctional movie - it's not the script I was hoping for but I know that if I tell him what I really want, he will run - and why should I even tell him - it hasn't really progressed since I met him in December. Would a woman with good self-esteem still be hanging around waiting for something more tangible to happen? If my own life was full and rich and busy and I was firing on all cylinders, I wouldn't be sitting around waiting for something to happen, but at the same time I am struggling to function - I have fallen for this man and it consumes me like a fire consumes oxygen...

I finally admit to myself, square on, that I need physical love - touch. I've crash landed. Gees I really do get excited over a few measly crumbs that are scattered in my direction. I will never forget a friend of mine telling me that she said to her boyfriend that she wants him to dazzle her. Enes arrives here with juice, melon and a little salad and I feel like a princess - what is wrong with me?

I go to bed and wonder what all the build up and anticipation was all about? I don't even know if we are remotely compatible as people - I don't even know him. I then go into a downward spiral. If I remove him from the picture - a man to hope and dream about, my life looks pretty empty and bleak, especially since I have also lost two friends along the way. What is there if I don't have Enes to hope about? He was a nice escape into an illusion of a bright future filled with companionship and a *cuddle partner.*

I am then reminded of the scene from the movie, The Matrix, where Neo is offered a red or blue pill. If he takes the blue pill he will forget that he ever saw the truth about the illusion of the Matrix. He will then be able to return, blissfully ignorant, to the unreality of the world, as we know it, being real. If he takes the red pill he will be given insight into all the illusions - reality exactly as it is. I had been given that same choice, symbolically, a long time ago. I had chosen the red pill because I wanted to explore the deeper meaning of life. My wise woman gets that I may have created this - all of it - including my so-called feelings for Enes. In this moment, I wish that I could *go* back and choose again - be born into a life of *ignorance is bliss* - just pop that blue tab and forget that I have looked deep into that tunnel of the delusion. I don't like to see so much. And a part of me wishes I had never met Enes!

I decide to message the *other guy*. I know he is crazy about me and maybe I should give him a chance. We get on so well. I don't think I want anything more than friendship with him but who knows - without all this angsty, *I've fallen for Enes* stuff - things could maybe evolve with Jay. Perhaps I really should be keeping my options open. I live an insular life. Should I really be excluding somebody I actually do like for a man who is so hot and cold and showing no signs of actually being attracted to me or wanting me to be a part of his day to day life?

## 21ˢᵗ April - Thursday

I have been having sexual fantasies about Enes making love to me. For the longest time that area of my womanhood was shut down. I went from being wholly in touch with my sexuality, in my youth, to closed off in recent years. I didn't even know if I could still get turned on. Since falling for Enes I have been masturbating again. My sexual centres are alive and well and thriving actually - getting wet, a possible issue after menopause, is no problem for me. I'm really enjoying my own self pleasuring again. What is it about this man that has awakened so much inside of me? Who the hell is he to me and why him? I want to know. I want answers.

I went online to send him a message and noticed that he was just online a few seconds before. I wonder who else he chats to. I wonder if there is another woman on the go and those familiar rejection thoughts push my buttons. I want to fast forward to the outcome - I want to get past this stage of irresolution. I want to know! I am losing patience with this enigmatic man - maybe it's because he's Turkish and from a different culture, that I have no clue what I am dealing with. I want physical and emotional with him. If I knew for certain he wouldn't abandon me, I would go for it right here and now. I would just go for it, no questions asked.

I sent a message then kind of felt weird about it. I think I should just back off. He replied and said he had been chatting to his heart broken niece, in Turkey and had a friend coming to visit from Ghana over the weekend - nice, so I guess that's another weekend where I will not get to see him. I wish I had my own people and places to go.

We chatted about my home made cream. What else can I talk about? I can't flirt. I can't tell him I have the *hots* for him and I get horny just thinking about him, so I chat about my cream instead. I had given him a sample and he seems to like it.

When I go to bed I am close to having an anxiety attack. I am beginning to realise that continuing in this long distance, half-hearted messaging and email based relationship is not good for me. I ask myself - if a friend was in this situation, what would I tell her? I would tell her that it looks like it's going nowhere with this guy. He is not making a move and you are investing too much of your energy in this. I understand that it's difficult to just cut when you have developed feelings for a man but you honestly deserve better than this. This guy is always busy with work or has his own plans that don't include you. He doesn't make time for you - not good enough; you know nothing about his life after all these months - not good enough. At the end of the day, when all is said and done, he is just not that into you and you want more so he's not good enough. No blame, not his fault. You can't force somebody to love you so the healthiest solution, if you really can't just be his friend, is to step out...

I wonder what he chats about to his niece in Turkey. I ask him about it? And decide it's late enough to go to bed.

*It is not, necessarily, that an emotionally unavailable man is not that into you. He is just not that into dealing with his own emotions. He didn't become like that after he met you or through meeting you. His style has been avoidance of any emotions that may make him feel uncomfortable for a much longer time, probably from childhood. If he senses that he could get close to you, he may become more avoidant than he would if he was in a friendship with a woman with absolutely no feelings of a possible romantic connection. It is so hard to tell. Whether he is or is not that into you, his behaviour will not, outwardly show you that he is into you so you will probably never know.*

## 22ⁿᵈ April - Full moon Friday

I am an emotional wreck. It is time to stop all the denial and own exactly how I feel. I can't go on pretending. I spent the morning in bed writing a letter to Enes that I don't intend ever sharing with him. In it, I express that I have feelings for him and I have been dishonest about just wanting to just be his friend. I doubt I will ever have the courage to actually send this and if I did, it could be the end of our friendship.

He sends me a message to say that he has sent me an email. I go to check my mail. He tells me he has been dealing with his niece, in Turkey, who fancied a man who she's had a friendship with for a long time. She was hoping to have a romantic connection with him in the future. Now this guy has met somebody else and she is devastated - he is giving her emotional support through it.

I am astounded by the *mirror* and the strong and powerful message the universe is sending me - the question I have been asking, do I continue with a dishonest friendship, is answered. The letter I am writing, confessing my feelings for him, at the exact same time, has to be sent - I have to tell him. If this isn't a sign, then what is it? I am being told to send it, to risk everything. I can't go on pretending. I could end up like his niece if I carry on like this - and I bet he won't be around to support me through it. *'It's all or nothing now,'* I tell myself. I have to do this. They talk about taking a *big swing* - it's courageous but it's risky - you can lose everything but if it works, you gain so much.

I type up a diluted version of the original from my journal. I don't want it to sound too intense. I say that perhaps he even has somebody else and that I may not even be a priority in his life. I press send and pray that the universe has done me a favour - that I will finally know for sure...

*Hi there*

*As I said in my message to you, I have been finding the synchronicity in the universe, absolutely mind blowing... not only in our situation but in many other instances. I have been receiving lots of clear signs recently with regards to questions about all sorts of things...*

*So pretty much while, I imagine, you were typing your email to me, I was writing something 'to you' in my journal (this is the honest truth...it's very weird actually. I usually write to myself, not to someone) ...I didn't really have any intention of sending it to you then your message came through that you had sent me an email and of course the 'mirror' here was really astounding... you will see what I mean when you read this letter I started writing to you in my journal...*

*From journal...BEFORE I GOT YOUR EMAIL.*

*I have been feeling very emotionally charged all week. The truth is that I 'lied to myself' about just wanting to be your friend. I am crazy about you! Maybe you can share your disassociation technique with me because I am feeling extremely 'disturbed' (LOL). I know the exact moment when I first felt this for you. It wasn't when we were sitting on that blanket, where we first met. It was a little bit later, after I'd had a chance to absorb it. You were standing outside, at the entrance of the house, chatting to someone. I turned and looked up at you and as I did that, you turned around and looked at me. It was so brief, it could easily have been missed and I doubt you even remember it.... but in retrospect I know, that was the 'ping' moment. Of course I have been in denial and I didn't own it right there and then...I just wanted new friends, remember - nothing more - that's how I lied to myself. 'Everything is so much more simple, without falling into this illusion,' is what I keep telling myself.*

*After I got your email*

*I was afraid that if I admitted to you that I didn't only see you as a friend, that you would run away...hehe...well, you could still run away but after hearing your nieces story, I think it's better, out in the open. We still have such a lot to learn about each other and I didn't want to put any expectation on it or have any type of agenda but I can't deny what I feel* **and it's better that I stop confusing myself by pretending,** *that I don't feel anything romantically for you.*

*I have no clue, where all this honesty will lead...I know you said you don't have time to make me a priority. You could even have somebody else you're interested in, for all I know...but I'm just being upfront about what I am feeling...that's all I can do really...and I'm very tempted to back out and not send this!*

*So there you have it...you can thank your niece for this...good or bad.*


*Blessings*

*Lilith*


He replies that he admires my honesty and the stand I am taking. He points out that it is not ordinary (a compliment) but he has been removed emotionally for many years and cannot see how a woman can fit into his life. He hardly has enough time in between work for his own life or to even visit me properly. He says there is no other priority (in other words, no other woman) and suggests that we just move on from this and continue our friendship.

I decide that I have one more card I can pull out from a magic hat. I have seen women use other men to make a guy jealous. It's never been my style and I don't like to play games but if he thinks there is a chance he may lose me, perhaps it will wake him up. I now feel like I have nothing to lose by telling him about Jay. My ego wants to rub it in that there is a man out there who is crazy about me if he doesn't want me - I am convinced he feels more for me than he is owning up to. What have I got to lose to tell him the honest truth about the other guy?

I write back and tell him about Jay. I tell him that I have no idea how I feel about him and was holding off on checking it out because I was hoping something would develop with him but now that this is out of the question, I think I should pursue something with this other guy. I tell him he is always welcome to come over any time.

His reply is rather short — *'cool catch up soon'*- It's not like him to have nothing to say, no words of wisdom or advice. I suspect he didn't enjoy the fact that there is another man waiting in the wings to step on to centre stage but he is never going to own up to that...

## 23ʳᵈ *April – Saturday*

I wake up to a different perception of my world. Enes is no longer a prospective boyfriend. I don't know how I got this so very, very wrong. All he can say is that I cleared some non-productive emotions and we should move on with our friendship. What I was trying to express seems to have *'whooshed'* through a wind tunnel between his ears and out the other side. I don't feel heard. Did he even get that I have strong feelings for him?

I sit and write another letter, in my journal, explaining how I don't want to land up in a crumpled heap like his niece - talking on the phone to a family member about my broken heart, in the future. I need to walk away - cut it - end it. It is going to end in pain for me. I'm the one with something to lose. He has nothing to lose.

I know I can't send him this letter. Do I really want to lose him altogether? I am in such an awkward position now. It seems like this man is one of the very few people in the universe, at this present moment, who I can relate to. I'm used to having him around to chat to. He has been my lifeline - now I want to push him away - but I know how this ends. Do I do it now or wait for the inevitable outcome further down the line? Even though I was filled with doubts a lot of the time, underneath it all I was quite convinced that he was into me romantically and all he needed was time but how much time and how much waiting was I prepared to do?

I write this letter to him in my journal…

*Hey Enes*

*I think you completely missed the message I felt the universe was sending me through the story you shared about your niece. If I continue to 'invest' in our 'friendship' I am certain, what I feel for you now, will grow over time. Every time I see you, I like you more. The likelihood is that I will always feel more for you than you do for me… more than just a friend. In my heart I will always have a longing to have more from you. So the way that I received the message from the universe, was a warning… a red flag. Your niece had a friendship with a guy and was hoping for a romantic connection some day in the future then he met somebody else…chances are that you will arrive at a point in your life where you meet somebody you would like to open your heart to and have a relationship with…where would that leave me…having a long distance conversation with a family member about how broken hearted I am – about how I had feelings for you all this time and now you have gone off with another woman. The only difference is that I will remember that the universe 'warned' me and I didn't listen. I will only have myself to blame for being so stupid. My father used to say that you don't only have to learn from your own mistakes…you can see them coming by learning from other people's mistakes too. This is clearly a case of 'you don't have to walk down that road because you have already been shown where it ends'.*

*It is very easy for you to say, let's move on from this because you don't have anything to lose emotionally but you do have a lot to gain from maintaining this friendship. I, on the other hand, know myself well…I invest a lot in people. You even told me, in an email that we should always make the proper investment type when we invest in people. Do you think it's appropriate to invest in you, knowing what I now know… that my feelings are one sided? I understand that we ultimately hurt ourselves by having unrealistic expectations but knowing this intellectually doesn't change the fact that my heart knows what it wants from this…I knew the moment I met you…I can't just dissociate and kill my feelings…*

*I don't really know what to do…maybe just some time and space…*

I know I won't send this…it's too much like an ultimatum. My inner child wants to lie in someone's arms and feel safe…I am so dejected I could scream. No part of me feels that I want to even look at a relationship with Jay. I can't go there while I have feelings for another man. Was my friendship with Enes enough? Why couldn't I just be satisfied with what I had? How ready was I, in reality, for a relationship anyway - I am so broken. What have I done? Have I lost him?

Perhaps I can rescue the situation before it's too late…I type this message *"I have landed with a bump today. I have been sooo down but will be okay. The thought of inviting someone new into my space is disturbing. I can't do it! I am just landing on my feet after what I've gone through and quite honestly don't have the energy to put myself out there. Our friendship was enough for me. What was I thinking? Maybe it was the full moon or something…good excuse! I know that you are pretty neutral and it makes no difference to you either way but just wanted to share this. I hope you are having a good weekend so far…."*

He hasn't replied and I may actually have lost him. I suppose if I'm so easy to walk away from then I wasn't really valued in the first place…

## 24ᵗʰ April - Saturday

I get a message from Enes telling me he is sorry about what I am going through and that I'm having a tough time.

He says that after kissing many frogs finding a prince will make it all worthwhile. He obviously has noooo idea how many frogs I have actually kissed and how disillusioned I actually am about men. I want to tell him that I have found my prince. I don't need to look any further - all he needs to do is open up his heart and kiss me. Of course I will not say this teenage stuff to him. We're grown-ups…

I reply with this -

*'For many years I have had the feeling that perhaps I am not meant to be in relationship and perhaps that isn't my journey anymore…too many frogs and lots of damage in my looong ago past. What I imagine in my mind is just an 'illusion'…there are no princes!!!! My body will not deal with any more pain….way too much for one*

*lifetime already!!!! It would take a 'miracle' for me to 'actually' do it again in reality! This has just been a reminder! Thank u for your kindness and your generosity of spirit and for 'getting me'...u are also not ordinary.*

Instead of distance he is now sending me emails telling me how he thinks I am built for relationship and then later tells me he has stomach cramps and at times like these it is not nice to be alone. I wish I was close enough to him to go over there and support him. I tell him I am here if he needs me. Why does this feel more like a new beginning than an ending? I don't realise that I am simply going back to square one again to start the process all over again - he is sending mixed signals. I have confessed I have feelings for him and instead of backing off it feels like he is coming in closer, *'Maybe he has feelings but is not ready to confront them'*, I tell myself. This man is just not behaving like someone who is completely shut off to a relationship with me.

Messages and emailing start becoming more frequent and although I am not seeing him physically we start covering a lot more ground in our communication. Instead of distance, we seem to be evolving - but still he is more a pen pal than a real man in my life but we seem to be much closer and we are sharing more in our emails.

---

**If your emotionally avoidant man values you, he will not want to lose you. He wants you in his life but it will always be on his terms. Don't expect an emotionally unavailable man to meet you halfway – there is only his way. Perhaps he is genuinely confused and doesn't understand exactly what it is he feels for you. He knows that if he gives you hope, he may just have to open himself up a little bit more and he may not be prepared to face that in himself. He has built a castle with high walls and a moat around himself for self preservation and protection. If he opens the castle door and welcomes you in, he is afraid that he will have to**

> *remove the armour coating that has taken him so long*
> *put on. He is afraid but he will never admit it.*

## 26th April - Monday

After all the loads of recent contact, I am once again thinking that Enes is perhaps more into me than he cares to admit - he really does seem to be more 'in' than before - very far from running away and my hope is renewed that I wasn't crazy after all.

Tomorrow is Freedom Day, in South Africa, and I just want to get out of the house - it's another holiday and no sign that Enes will grace me with his presence. I can't bear the thought of sitting around wondering if he will ever make space for me in his life. I phone my aunt and ask her if I can visit for the night. I want to go past the wholesaler and buy some bulk cream jars for my natural cream. It seems to be getting good results with abnormal skin growths and I want to market it. I pack a bag and my laptop and head into town. It's a very run down part of town and it depresses me to see so much desperation around me - people on the streets pulling recycling carts so they can earn some cash to put a little bit of food in their bellies.

I was feeling very wound up inside. I wanted Enes to want me - I longed for the opportunity to spend time with him. I wanted him to catch a glimpse of my day to day life - to see what we could potentially be like together. I had a taste and liked him more every time I saw him but the gaps between those times grew wider and with it my hope of more with him, was dying. I know I can't force him to want to make me a priority in his life. He has been using my cream and said that this was my way of sharing my healing abilities and he has picked up that I'm a natural healer. I know he is rooting for my cream and for me but that seems to be the limit of what he is prepared to give me - a distant nudge of support.

When I confided in my aunt, about Enes, she said he seems to be a dead end and that I was wasting my time with him then my cousin visited and she said that a man should always be more into you than you are into him. Their feedback, although somewhat limited because they didn't fully understand the dynamics, felt like yet another reminder - a slap from the universe to remind me, yet again, that my illusion of being with this man, was a hopeless unreality.

## 27ᵗʰ April - Tuesday

Enes messaged me this morning to say he had sent me an email, which is a reminder of why I am still holding on to some form of hope. I told him I was at my *other mommy* - my late mother was her baby sister. I said she loved having me around and was lonely after her soul mate of 65 years had passed away. I said she missed him terribly.

He replied saying — imagine being in my shoes with no kids and no family and how lucky I was to have a relevant person like this in my life. Suddenly my heart goes out to him. It was sad. It struck me that he was really making himself vulnerable for a change. He seldom expresses anything remotely about how he actually *feels* about anything. My first instinct was to tell him that he could have a ready-made family right here and now!! I had a good chuckle to myself about this. If he was able to get the humour in it, it would be fun to share it but then I realised he probably wouldn't see it as funny - you can have it all if you want it. Here it is, come and get it! The twins will love you - my son will get on well with you - what are you waiting for??? My family would embrace him - they would love a man to come into my life and see me happy for a change. But of course there is just the small little detail that he doesn't actually want a relationship with me and has never even invited me to his home.

I would give anything to include him in my life but he's making it so very, very difficult. I wondered if the early email was perhaps going to lead to him making a plan to see me today but that was a long shot and I can't even begin to assume what is really going through this man's mind. I sent a watered down version of how family aren't always our blood relatives - I have soul family that I consider family to me - it's a hint but a very cryptic message. I just can't be upfront with this man...

I check my email and he speaks about letting go and quotes Einstein who says that we must let our emotions go like balloons so we can rise above all the mess down below.

I spend another night with my aunty. I feel *cushioned* here in her company - at least I have somebody to talk to, cook for - share with.

> *I suspect that emotionally unavailable men are of the sensitive kind, now referred to as empaths or highly sensitive. To get along and survive in a man's world, they have had to suppress their sensitivity and have learned to cover it up by creating layer upon layer of self protection. Perhaps this began from childhood where boys weren't allowed to cry or show emotion without being ridiculed - perhaps even by their own fathers who wanted them to toughen up and become real men, according to their own perception of what a real man is. Emotions became responsible for embarrassment and loaded with negative connotations. The root of emotions is associated with fear – emotions are associated with feeling disturbed as they become seen as the cause of unnecessary pain.*

## 29th April – Friday

When I got back home from my aunt, I decided to send Enes an email in reply to his message about trying to imagine being in his family-less shoes - and yes, I felt really awful about it. What exactly was he trying to say to me - had I misread everything and was he actually wanting *me* to reach out more???

I started the email pointing out that some cell messages warranted a response. I said I understand that messages can't go on and on but sometimes I feel that my messages to him are left hanging (there had been a couple messages that had been ignored)…I had actually been wanting to point this out to him and thought I'd just mention it here.

Mostly the email was to tell him that I would include him more in my life if he wanted it but he seemed to have lots of friends and I thought he was content with his life the way it is. I said that I spend a lot of weekends alone and I don't have many friends left around the area - they had all moved on. (I have friends all over the world now…it seems most of them got out, to better lives, at some point). I thought my email was being kind. He had mentioned something to me about when he realised it was too late to have children, that there was a certain amount of regret around this, at the time, so I mentioned this.

He had clearly not taken kindly to the lecture about replying to messages, when he sent his email response. He said that it would better not to place him in a frame to avoid disappointment within the friendship - it seems a bit drastic and really put the lid back on that jam jar - and I had just opened it up and dipped into it - now he was *warning* me that if I go there, he will not stick around to help me eat it - so much for me thinking he was actually reaching out.

I felt a bit angry - so what exactly was that all about? I always end up feeling confused, almost violated but on the other hand he also shares some amazing wisdoms about our perceptions and how our wounds help us grow on other levels. I know he quite fancies himself as the guru and I really love all his wisdoms - it's just the relationship stuff that I still find so bewildering. His philosophies and his wisdoms are what I love about this man - the question is do I continue to stick around for the other half of him that pushes me away?

## *May*

### *1ˢᵗ May - Sunday*

I wake up in an okay space. I've wanted to make some type of decision regarding Jay. He still sends me such lovely messages that are always so good for my ego. I sent him a message asking him if he's okay with just friendship. He says that's good for him but I know how that feels - he is actually in the same position I am in with Enes - surely it can't feel great for him.

Enes sent me a message yesterday saying that I must just let my emotions go so that I can find some peace with a whole lot of balloon emoticons. I'm so tired of him negating my feelings. I decided to be real about it - that my emotions are my guidance system and they make me the caring, sensitive person I am - I don't want to get rid of them! Then I decide to be obnoxious and say *'Peace is for sissy's'*. I am never sure how he will take my tongue in cheek humour - there is still a language barrier but I actually didn't care in that moment. He didn't reply. Like I said, we always seem to go back to the beginning to start the process all over again. I feel so utterly ALONE!

*I write this in my diary…the universe supports my need for that one person who always has my back…that one person who not only gets me but is crazy about me. The universe supplies me with everything I need and want… a man who mutually wants to develop a partnership with me… to build and grow together… to love, to touch… two pieces of a whole, the yin curled up in the enclaves of the yang and vice versa. It flows. It is easy and uncomplicated… we flow along this river of life of together. I deserve him and he deserves me. We want the same things. Our needs are congruent with each other's needs. I am allowed to have what I want! I allow myself to accept this good into my life now.'*

## 2nd *May - Monday*

I just gave myself a very good talking to while I relaxed in a nice aroma, ylang, ylang scented bath. I sent Enes an email earlier saying I didn't want to have a long distance relationship with somebody who lives just down the frigging road (I didn't use those words exactly). What the f*&k am I doing this for? I am wasting precious living time writing emails to somebody who never bothers to get in his car and visit me. I could have written a whole new book by now. This man hasn't contributed anything to my life in reality. I don't want this. I really don't want this! If our feelings were mutual I would say a big YES to him but they're not so I need to put out a big Nooo to the universe on this one and let him go. It's bullshit, pathetic and degrading. It has to stop - *put yourself out of your misery, woman and end it now - just stop!*

I deserve to have the man I'm crazy about, mutually crazy about me - if he's not then I don't want it. That's it. It's not complicated. It's a no brainer. I'm feeling incredibly pissed off right now. Why did I attract an unavailable man into my life? What's wrong with me?

I decide to do some proof reading on my book. I thought the book was proof read enough but my daughter found some mistakes and I was astounded so she sent me some pencilled pointers to correct. The section of the book I'm working on focuses on the question - are our lives dictated by destiny or choice? I start off by referring to this passage about a frog that thinks spring is, literally, around the corner - and how many of us live our lives in expectation of something that may happen in the future and miss out on being in the present moment :-

*'I once bought my children a book about a young frog, still green and wet behind the ears, who overhears that spring is just around the corner. This naïve, little 'froggie', goes on a mission to look around every corner, to see if spring is there. Most of us live our lives like this, in a perpetual state of illusionary 'wishful thinking', chasing after the pot of gold at the end of the rainbow, the beautiful colour spectrum of the actual rainbow, passing us by. This frog can be forgiven as youth is meant to be full of searching and seems to guarantee a form of hope that something better, is tangible, if only it can be found. After all, it is just around the next corner, yet in doing so we forget to put ourselves wholly in the present moment, by projecting our happiness and contentment, on to a state we hope to find ourselves in, sometime in the future'* – The Other Side of My Reflection by Lilith White.

I decide to email this section of my book to Enes. He hasn't seen any of the book yet and I think this is relevant to the conversations, we've been having in our emails, so I copy it to email and send it.

### 3ʳᵈ May – Tuesday

Before I even opened my eyes, tears were streaming down my cheeks. I hate admitting how unhappy I feel – I believe I should be more evolved and beyond all of this *stuff* but the word *'should'* is always followed by a guilt trip - so I allowed myself to cry - to really cry. Losing Enes - or the fantasy of Enes - is a loss even though I never even got to first base with him. People seem to be of the opinion that if you didn't sleep with a man, you don't have a right to grieve for him - like feelings only exist once he's claimed you by semen injection. Before copulation, you are a nobody!

A message comes through from Enes late evening, *'Thanks for that sharing - sent an email'*. My heart expands. So much for letting him go. I sent a message back saying I hoped he was having a good evening and that it was nearly his bedtime. He said, *'that's right'* and I said *'sleep tight'* - usually that's it with him but after me scolding him about some messages warranting a response and him lecturing me about not putting him in a box, he confirms that he took note by replying, *'tx you too'*.

I suddenly feel *heard* by him and hope is renewed that this could possibly end up going somewhere - tonight he is hot - tomorrow he could be cold. My heart expands some more. I feel elated - oh, my gosh I really do have it bad for this man. A thought suddenly runs through my mind that this man could actually be in love with me - whether or not he admits this to himself, he sometimes comes across as a man who is smitten. It's so very confusing. This is the first time I even consider this as an option – what if he's actually in love with me?

I notice that every time I mention my other friend, the man who is actually hitting on me, he says very little or does not reply at all. He responds to everything else except for any mention of Jay, who he pretends does not even exist.

So I go to check my mail. He has sent me an incredible email. It is not personal but very profound - he talks about how, in the Islamic culture, they give acknowledgement and appreciation for what they already have. I read it about three times. It blew my mind and confirms for me, yet again, what I actually see in this man - he is different - he is a deep thinker - he is wise. We must count our blessings and give thanks for what we have and only then do we ask for what we would like to have in our lives. At first I thought he was talking generally then I thought, *'Hey wait a minute, perhaps there is more of a personal message hidden in there'*. I felt like a spoilt ungrateful child, dissatisfied with what I already have with this man. He is a precious gem - worth so much to me just the way he is. In that moment, I felt absolutely blessed to have Enes in my life - the orb in my heart swells some more and I fall a little bit deeper for him - dare I call it *'in love'*.

## 4ᵗʰ May – Wednesday

This morning I woke up feeling so centred in my being. I remember feeling this so profoundly when I visited Turkey like everything about the place and the people resonated with me - the respect for life and others, the way the young man on the boat, Ali, handled the drunken uncouth brat from Australia who had no respect for them or their culture. I had never felt this anywhere else before. Enes had touched on Muslim culture in his email to me and something about this resonated deeply in my being - I wonder about past life connections and a part of me feels an alignment with Enes that goes beyond the *'story'* I am telling myself in this lifetime about him.

I then start thinking about my pattern, in recent years of going for unavailable men. I realise that if they can't be in a relationship with me, for whatever the different reasons have been, then I never have to know whether or not it would have succeeded - a bit like buying a lottery ticket and never checking to see if your numbers came up - you never know the outcome and you can remain in pure denial. Again I ask myself, *'Is there also a part of myself that has become unavailable?'*

Momentarily I have the thought, *"I'm in love...I'm in love!"* What has been intangible to me, now becomes tangible. I had been too afraid to say or think those words - fallen for him sounds much less risky. I don't really know exactly what *in love* means anymore. I thought I knew what it all meant, in my youth, but now I honestly don't know. All I have to go on is what I'm feeling and it feels like love to me - in love with Enes.

I don't hear from him today - a whole day without any contact. It strikes me again how weird it is that this man is so much part of my life and not at all a part of it at the same time.

*I found this quote online, written by an emotionally unavailable man on the blog singleblackmale.com. It is so to the point and is an honest confession from an emotionally unavailable man:*

*"They figure if they can determine why we're emotionally unavailable, then they can just help us address that issue and all will be right with the world. Still though, no matter how stern our warnings, no matter how many times we tell you that our emotional unavailability is serious and not a game, you still find a way to allow yourselves to fall to the point of no return."*

*This emotionally unavailable man clearly doesn't get the concept that falling for him was not necessarily an intellectual decision... and that his warnings are futile in the face of matters of the heart - would us woman, rather have fallen for an available man who loved and adored us and wanted us just as much as we wanted him — yes, of course we would have.*

*It is always a good idea to question our underlying patterns and ask why we would chose to sabotage ourselves in this way, but no matter how much we question our underlying motives, sometimes it's as simple as the heart wants what the heart wants. My heart just knew what it wanted and it was this specific man — emotionally unavailable or not - him and nobody else I knew at that present time.*

## 5ᵗʰ May - Thursday

The clock is ticking on the wall and I am starting to feel a no contact gap - my world seems to revolve wholly around the distant contact with this man. It's been nearly two days and I wonder whether he also feels a gap when we don't chat. I know that *breathing space* is good. A message comes through that he has been working late and has sent me an email. I go to check the message and it's a motivational questionnaire that I, kind of assumed, he wrote up for his team at work.

I am grateful that he thought of me in the *'busyness'* of his day. He had asked me, in a previous email, why I thought I had attracted an unavailable man and I threw the question right back at him - have you asked yourself why you attracted me into *your* life. He hadn't answered that question - I doubted he would ever answer that. I read through the questionnaire and realised that I had no *clever* answers. I am so over and beyond trying to slot my life into some philosophical new agey *'you create your own reality'* type mindset.  A part of me experienced a numb neutrality. Maybe he thinks his sole purpose, in my life, is to teach me something. Perhaps that's how he explains away his feelings for me... *'Ahh, haa, now I understand why I'm drawn to her...I must have come into her life to be her teacher'* - that would be a nice, safe, neat little box to explain away our attraction to each other.

I realise how little he knows me - does he honestly think I have never come across Wayne Dyer or the likes of other *'power of the mind'* gurus? He makes assumptions that I need this stuff and avoids the real question - why did you attract me into your life? It's a bit frustrating and I have to own that it's not the question avoidance I want to hear right now. At the same time, it's so incredibly thoughtful that he had thought about me in the middle of his busy work day. I guess I may have been right about him feeling a gap and this was his way of reaching out and closing it - the thought crosses my mind again — *'maybe he is actually in love with me'*. Does it matter that he wants to teach me something. There are many things I can and want to learn from him. I love that about him.

I entered this quote in my journal from the movie Something's Gotta Give. I love movie quotes and this is a 'goodie…'

Erica, played by Diane Keeton is a woman in her fifties. She meets, Harry, a single, confirmed bachelor who has never married or had children. She is thrown into a sexual relationship with him and falls for him, but Harry can't commit to anything (he is clearly an emotionally unavailable man),

*"I like you" he says*

*And she says, "Yeah but I like you, love you. I do love you - what was I thinking - my life has been turned upside down - you know the life I had before you - I knew how to do that. I could do that forever. But now look at me. What am I going to do?"* (She is an emotional wreck just like me).

*He replies, "The truth is that I don't know how to be a boyfriend."*

***Emotionally unavailable men are creatures belonging to their very own category - they probably don't know why they do what they do or don't do what they don't do - and how does a girl have any clue how to handle this strange thing she is faced with - walk away or try and break through - walk away or try and break through. Keep knocking on that door - chances are nobody will open it but what if they do? What if one day he wakes up and lets you in. That is the dilemma — what if he one day decides to let you in…***

Tonight I still feel a certain amount of neutrality - I hope this almost numb feeling lasts and I am released from this torment of completely losing my balance over an elusive beloved that has no idea that I do actually love him.

## 6th May - Friday

I decided today that I am *allowed* to feel that a motivational questionnaire, as a form of communication, is not good enough - sure it's sweet and could be his way of showing that he cares but once again I feel like he's scattering out a few crumbs for me to peck at. I have many tools in my toolbox to fix myself up and if he had taken the time, in his free time, to get to know me, face to face, then he would know this about me. If this is all he has to offer, I accept it graciously. I bless him for it but I seem to be in the habit of being so grateful to people for such a small amount of effort like that's as much as I deserve. I want people to stretch themselves for me as I do for them. I am not a mediocre person and I do not have to settle for mediocrity - show me you care by being present in my life - show up - be there! It doesn't have to be fireworks - just some basic one on one human interaction would be good enough. If you want to be a part of my life, please show up with something real and tangible.

*This is the wise woman talking – rare moments like these when your self-esteemed woman tells you exactly what you want. This is when you really stop and listen. This aspect of you knows the answer to all of your questions. She knows what she wants and she knows that she can have it. In moments like these I suggest you get out a pen and paper and write these affirmations on 'post-it's' or any bit of paper you can find and paste them around your space so that you do not forget yourself and what it is that you are really looking for...*

My empowered moment is short lived. I decide to clean the house to clear the space and nearly have an anxiety attack. The thought of losing him clogs my throat — I want to curl up in a ball and cry. I needed this dream - I needed a lifeline and there he was. My evolved self *gets* it all - he doesn't want to be limited to the picture I want to frame him in but that makes my *little girl self* feel vulnerable and threatened. I just want to withdraw back into my reclusive little cocoon where I felt safe, where I felt a certain amount of security and balance like that woman in, Something's Gotta Give says, *I knew how do to my life before I met you - now look at me*! I actually can't do this with this guy anymore - it places a restriction on me - what I am and what I am not allowed to ask for. The irony is that he is actually the one, placing a box around our friendship and labelling it according what makes him feel safe - and making our relationship conditional…

## 7<sup>th</sup> May - Saturday

Today I had this thought about love sickness. I know, as an evolved woman, this idea is perfectly ludicrous but I was curious because I felt utterly dissipated with no energy whatsoever. I feel sick in the pit of my stomach. I am astounded to find that love sickness is now a recognised psychological disorder. It didn't occur to me that perhaps I was simply ill. Of course, if you understand the mind body connection on a deeper level, you also understand that there is really no difference between the two and possibly on a purely simplistic level, this relationship with this man has now become unhealthy for me. Oh, my gosh, I am a mess - *I have an illness called Love Sickness*!

I phoned my girl friend, Annie, in tears. I have got it so bad for this man and I have absolutely no idea what I'm going to do about it. I just wanted it all to go away. In that moment I honestly wished I'd never met him - that I could go back to my silly little, safe life where I had found a small amount of peace and sanity. I sent him a message saying that I appreciated the questionnaire. I didn't know what else to say - I wanted to be real - ask him how I answer the question, '*what excites and motivates you?*' - do I tell him that my first inclination to answer that question was, **"YOU DO"** and then I went completely blank - how could I tell him that besides him, nothing excites me. He would realise how dysfunctional I am. The secret would be out that my goals and dreams have been dead and buried for the longest time - that without this *love creation*, my life is completely devoid of any aspirations. That would be a big turn off...

It would be better to just back off completely but that just made me feel worse. I owed him a proper mindful email response to his questionnaire like I have always done - after all, none of this was actually his fault. He was just being nice. I sent a message apologising for not sending him a proper response - he was so used to me being engaging and verbal in emails. He replied that I was going through a transition and it was never easy...

And weekends have become a mammoth challenge for me because, in the back of my mind, I know that he could see me if he really wanted to and it's *in my face* that he's not making an effort and that translates into - he's just not that into you otherwise he would be making an effort – it truly sucks.

Later on I realised that I was actually physically ill. I sent a message saying I thought I had a bug. He said that if it persists I must see an expert on Monday. I felt much better having some contact with him and now had nausea, the runs and no appetite. We had nice chatty communication – tonight he's warm.

## 8th May - Sunday

It was Mother's Day and I wouldn't be going anywhere today. I sweated it out the whole night. All I wanted was to hear from Enes. I convinced myself he wouldn't even bother - why would he - he doesn't really care about me and it was all my fault because he would have picked up that I had backed off. I sent him an energetic apology through the telepathic airwaves. What was wrong with me? This man was kind. Even if he's not in love with me, he still shows me that he cares. Not long after this, a message came through wishing me a *Happy Mother's Day* and asking how I was doing. I am an idiot. At least somebody, other than my son, is thinking about me today (my daughter lives in the UK and Mothering Sunday is a different day over there so she often doesn't know it's Mother's Day here – not that I'm big on the special days hype but it is always nice to know you're thought of).

Lucien came round and we moved the TV into my room. It didn't work so we moved everything back again. I had quinoa - forced it down and my tummy didn't run. Later, I ate a slice of tart and it was all systems go for a slice of toast. I'm on the mend.

A thought crossed my mind of something Enes had said along the lines of don't have any lack thoughts and it will happen in time – '*I must listen to the wise one*', I thought!

## 10ᵗʰ May - Tuesday

The thing with falling in love, is that you open up your heart. Mine has been closed for so long. I have opened up the flood gates to everything that has been dammed up inside of me - my heart is now open and all the pain, surfacing hurts so very, very much. I found a door to the room with no view and opened it up. I can't contain it anymore. It has to be set free. I have gone ahead of myself with this *in love* thing with Enes. All I had wanted was to take baby steps into a new friendship with him and look what I have done.

My dear, old friend, Annie, called to have a chat and asked me round for dinner tomorrow evening - somebody is actually being a real friend for a change. We chatted about this *falling for a man* stuff. I said maybe I had fallen for him because I had made a decision based on criteria. I told her that I admire him and there haven't been many men in my life who I actually admire. She said that I am a goddess and if I really want him, I can have him. She said I must be the Leo queen that I am.

After the conversation I pondered on what she had said and asked the universe to tell me, '*What I must do next?*' I went to make some food and as I closed the kitchen curtains, I noticed the moon hanging in the yonder heavens. It was the same *half fullness* it was the last time I walked Enes to his car to say goodbye - gosh, it had been four whole weeks - plus a day, I corrected myself - of almost daily communication but there was no real Enes in sight. The moon, half full with expectation, the last time he was here, was now half empty with broken dreams of something that had not materialised - I berated myself for having that thought. I didn't want to freak myself out - not tonight. I was working on being the goddess - perhaps in this situation the goddess is just silent - she gives it space.

I felt like doing an I-Ching but I didn't have my I-Ching book with me. I decided to open up my own, published book, The Other Side of my Reflection, on any page and see what it said. I was astounded — *"To believe that you have the power to end your pre-ordained Karmic relationships, is as painfully ignorant as to believe that all you are is a body that dies and disintegrates leaving nothing behind except a heap of potential compost for Mother Earth to disseminate and de-compose. There is a saying that, 'It's not over until it's over,' which suggests that a relationship, still cluttered up with unfinished business is only ended when the purpose of your coming together has been fulfilled. It is not up to us, with our limited capacity to extend ourselves through timelessness into past lifetimes, to decide the fate of our connections in future incarnations. The best you can do is ride the river like a surfer handing himself over to the power of the sea, using his acquired skills from previously learned lessons, to guide him safely to shore."* - The Other Side of My Reflection by Lilith White.

I decided I had to allow the universe to provide a clear answer. This message from my own book had been profound but I still felt completely confused. I know that karmic relationships need to be lived out in order to clear past baggage but I just longed for it to be simple for a change - boy meets girl - they get it together and face whatever comes, holding hands - simple. Sometimes I wished there was a genie you could ask for advice. I asked my dad, even though he had passed. I never asked his advice when he was alive - now I wished there was a daddy around that I could speak to.

## 11ᵗʰ May – Wednesday (a month since I saw Enes)

It was early and I was still half asleep when my phone beeped - it was a message from Enes. I felt instantly nauseous even though I felt extremely exultant to hear from him. He asked how I was doing? I am convinced that we are mirroring each other, even though the part of me that wants to keep myself secure doesn't want to believe it. Had he picked up energetically that I had planned to remain silent? He had clearly woken up thinking of me. It felt good.

I went to visit my boys. They were tearing around the house on their scooters. I decided to send Enes a couple of photos of them then as I sent them, I kind of regretted it - I don't know why. We had started the day off on a high note but he didn't respond to the pics and I felt weird about it. This is always what it's like with him - it feels like he's reaching out and then when I try to get a flow going, he blocks it - and I end up feeling like an idiot for not keeping a more healthy distance like I had planned to do. Then I start imagining all sorts of shit because the reality is that he has a secret life that I know nothing about - does he hire whores, I wonder. It's not like this thought hadn't entered my mind before - and if he does, is that so bad? He's a man with needs and money. Maybe that just suits him and keeps him emotionally unavailable. I don't see anything too wrong with it actually but energetically it's probably not cool because sex with prostitutes is purely on a physical, lower energy plain.

My father came up for me again when I washed my sheets. I use the down duvet he used in the old age home and his name is on it - then my friend Clint messaged me a link. He was looking for a place to stay and one of the property advertisers had the same name as my dad and he asked if I think he's trying to contact me. It was pretty weird. I wondered if perhaps he actually was…

## 12ᵗʰ May - Thursday

I awoke from a hectic dream. I had thought it was possible that Enes is actually into men. A guy who was staying with him called me to tell me he was *fucking other men*. I was really freaked out - even if I had created this dream from my own sub-conscious, surely the fact that he has not allowed me into his world says it all - I still know very little about him.

### Later

I messaged Enes to ask him if he was okay because I'd had a hectic dream (obviously I didn't go into detail). I thought perhaps I should just check in with him just in case the message in the dream was something else. I was feeling so overwhelmed and exhausted. He said he was good and had been swimming at the gym. I was relieved.

I woke up in the middle of the night and needed to get this down. I had another disturbing dream. Two of my old friends were now in contact with Enes. My one friend had stolen my first love when I was a teenager and she had gone on to marry him, to be abused by him and had divorced him. It was all so long ago but in the dream I was screaming at her that what she had done to me was wrong. Enes was now in their lives, giving my other friend's daughter lifts to school.

I am now completely distraught. Clearly this man is no longer good for me. Messaging and emails are not a *real relationship* and it's obviously playing on my mind - he is free to do as he pleases - I am not a priority in his life. Now more than ever, I need to make a decision regarding where to from here... I need to take back my power and the only way to do this is to stop waiting for him to make a move. I have to choose - do I remove myself from his life completely?

The only positive about the second dream was that it made me realise that the first dream had not been based in reality. My own mind was sending me distress signals in my sleep but the *stories* around them were not real. I also realised I have been carrying deep scars from the heart break in my youth - betrayal and desertion was in the forefront - and my contact with Enes was pushing these buttons.

The only way that I could continue contact with this man was if we could have real time together to get to know each other better - but I couldn't *force* face to face contact with him. It wasn't up to me. He had been to my home three times. I had cooked him amazing food and there was no reciprocation - so much for being the goddess - goddess my ass. I was just being an idiot. Tomorrow is Friday - any plans to see Enes over the weekend - I doubt that very much - just not good enough!

> *A relationship with an emotionally unavailable man is often very simple in his mind. He appreciates your company when he feels like it. He stays in touch with you because you both enjoy the contact. You talk about your outlooks on life, what you enjoy doing in your leisure time and perhaps talk generally about relationships with friends and family. You never talk about what you feel for each other. You do not discuss how long it will go on for and it is never clear if you will do anything together, whatsoever, in the future.*

## 13ᵗʰ May - Friday

Today I had a wonderful *girlie day* with Lisa. She had called me to say she missed me and invited me to go to a health spa and then out for lunch. I am not one to carry grudges and I forgave her instantly.

My massage therapist was incredible. Some people just have that magic touch. After the massage I was starving. Since ICU I have not really had an appetite but I felt like I could eat a horse. We went to a place called The Ocean Basket, a food chain that does fairly good fish. Enes had messaged me earlier and I messaged him back from there telling him I had gone for a massage with a friend and was having lunch.

When I got home, I felt so incredibly good. I had had an awesome day. I wanted to share my *feel good vibe* so I messaged him to tell him about my day and I added *'I'm so pleased I have you in my life'*. I also mentioned that our mutual friend, Kendall, was visiting from the UK and she had mentioned a get together dinner on Tuesday night.

I waited for his response thinking the message warranted a reply. The lack of response felt like a slap in the face. I was feeling great for the first time in a long time - I guess it was just a little bit too personal for his liking - he didn't want me to think of him as in my life probably - just another reminder that this emotionally unavailable man is so avoidant that it makes me want to scream.

## 14ᵗʰ May - Saturday

I woke up thinking that I need to start speaking up for myself and stop being the victim. I had said *I am so pleased I have you in my life* - should I rephrase that and send a message saying, *I am painfully aware that you are not in my life like IN MY LIFE - I'm so please I have you as a pen pal!* I decide to go on and type something along these lines and he is typing. It felt pretty synchronistic and stopped me in my tracks, from sending it. His response was pretty general in nature. I got the feeling he had been mulling over his reply. He said that I was showing signs of healing and also said he had heard about the dinner on Tuesday.

We had quite a chatty messaging session. I asked him his star sign, saying that I didn't like to limit people to their sign but I was interested - he came back with Gemini - go figure - yes, never try and pin a Gemini down and worse if they are a self confessed emotionally unavailable one. His birthday is the 6th of the 6th. Something else struck me after our chat. I had studied numerology many years ago and I had noted that the property number, where I stay, is six. It was 213 which is a six. I had also noted that my cottage, although there were only four cottages on the property had a six on the door and a six on the key ring. I was surrounded by six energy in my home.

There was no mention of maybe getting together over the weekend which got under my skin AGAIN. I was beginning to realise that I couldn't go on like this - putting myself through so much pain. It was time for me to make a decision about what I was going to do to get my life back on track.

I went to the shops and while I was standing in front of the big, ripe juicy melons and deciding which one to buy, a message came in from an old friend of mine who lives in Cape Town. She told me she had met someone two months previously (she got divorced years ago and had been single for a few years). She was now happily in a relationship with a man who treated her like a princess. In that moment it felt like the bottom had dropped out of my world. My reaction was completely and utterly irrational. I started shaking and tears poured down my face. I should be happy for her - I was happy for her but it was such an overwhelming moment of realisation - she had known him two months and he was right in there with her. She deserved it but I felt a deep, envy, not of her but for the situation. What was wrong with me? I have known Enes a whole lot longer than that and I'm still kidding myself it could be going somewhere. I guess it was this realisation that finally whacked me into the plain, irrefutable truth - IT WAS GOING NOWHERE WITH ENES.

## 15ᵗʰ May - Sunday

I woke up feeling like I had fallen off a cliff and was now dangling over the edge by a thin thread - another Sunday in another empty weekend. A decision had to made about what was ultimately going to be good for me, moving forward. I needed to focus on my own life and end this love sickness type of madness or whatever it was I had so bad - *'I'm a grown woman - enough of behaving like a teenager'*.

In all this time, I had never blamed Enes for anything. He had never made me any false promises, he hadn't even made any innuendos that could have been misconstrued as misleading me - he had behaved like the perfect gentleman – too much like the perfect gentleman - and a Mr. Nice Guy of note, except for sometimes being a bit hard of heart and callous about my emotions but other than that, I could not fault him. I couldn't blame him for not falling in love with me. He had done nothing wrong but I had to make a decision about what was going to serve me, to further my own self growth and happiness in my future and being in this *association* with Enes wasn't uplifting.

As if he had read my mind, a message comes through that he had had a product launch and had worked from ten on Saturday night until three in the morning. I know this is how it goes with his job. He has had product launches before. It was almost like he was apologising to me without really knowing what he was apologising for. Why would a man who is not interested in me be doing this - that is the question? I have these moments where I think that he is actually just as much in love with me as I am with him but he's just not admitting it - either just to me or to himself as well.

## 17th May - Tuesday

Enes sends me a message to ask if I'm going to the dinner tonight. I reply that I am but I don't yet have the full details. He says he has them and would I like to go with him seeing as he is on my way. In the conventional world of romance, with a regular guy, this could not be misconstrued as a date but this is not a regular type of man who takes women out. My friend Kendall told me she has never seen him with a woman, in the four or so years she has known him, so this small, usually mundane invitation, felt like a biggie. He was inviting me to go with him and be seen with me in public. It felt more like a date.

I was beside myself. Could this be the breakthrough I've been waiting for? Dare I even hope for that? I contacted Lisa (we had rekindled our friendship) and asked her opinion - she said it sounded like a big step and felt that it was kind of like a date. I asked her if I could come over for a hair trim. I needed some moral support and I wanted to look gorgeous.

After my visit to her, I spent the rest of the afternoon slowly getting ready. I was more nervous about it than I cared to admit. This was make or break for me! I had already considered that the dinner could be a turning point and perhaps I would start stepping out from there. Something had to give and this was going to be crunch time.

I left home looking and feeling amazing but extremely nervous. Enes had sent his address and it was going to be the first time I had seen his home. He said I should message him from the car as he was still at work and would leave when I'm on my way - this, in itself, seemed a bit odd. I knew where he worked and to come home first, he would be driving in the opposite direction from the restaurant. In order for us to go together, he had to backtrack to come home first. The get together was much closer to his work. In other words, he was going out of his way to go with me.

He was already home when I got there. His place was clearly a bachelor pad - a little bit uninspiring and could have done with a woman's touch. It was nice enough but he was definitely not an interior decorator. There was a pile of dirty dishes in the kitchen that actually made me feel more comfortable about him - at least he wasn't obsessive - I couldn't handle that. Neat freak men are scary! He mentioned that he had a dinner party the night before with *the boys* because his old friend had visited him from Cape Town. He went out of his way to show me a group photo of the gang, taken on his phone. I was a bit confused. He seemed to be making a point - the thought crossed my mind again, that perhaps he was into men.

He said he wanted to wait for the traffic to die down before we left so we sat and chatted. I guess it was really not very bright of me but I asked him again if he was gay. He said he wondered if that's what people thought because he doesn't chase after women. He said he had never even thought about being with a man. He mentioned something about being sexually active but that was different from a relationship. He seemed quite relaxed talking about it and I never got the sense that my question had upset him.

He told me that he had spent ten years in and out of relationships (it sounded like my life story) and then the last eight years or so had Adrenal Fatigue and had been single. He said he had never taken a woman back to Turkey and wondered if his family also thought there was something wrong with him. I told him I had only lived with one man since my husband's death when I was twenty seven. Does that mean that there is something wrong with me too? He said it's different for women. Men are supposed to be the hunters and do people think just because he doesn't hit on women, he is abnormal.

Just before we left he told me that he just wanted to let me know that he had bumped into Dona, the same Dona that had been trying to get him to a social event, through me, since the first dinner party. I asked him if she'd asked for his number. He hesitated. Yes, she did. I didn't get the feeling he was interested in her. It felt more like he was letting me know so that I could trust him.

We left for the restaurant and he took a round-a-bout way to show me the previous place where he had lived. When we arrived at the venue and got out of the car, his vibe changed. Maybe the reality of arriving with me had suddenly dawned on him. I'm not exactly sure what it was but he kind of walked ahead of me as if he was leaving me behind - but then stopped and waited for me, to go through the door first. I was greeted by Dona's smiling face when I walked in. She was sitting next to an empty seat. When she greeted me with, *"This is a nice surprise,"* I realised that she was expecting Enes to come alone and the empty seat had been reserved for him. It was awkward to say the least.

Enes directed me into the *Enes, expectant chair* and squeezed into another one they put at the end of the table - sort of next to me.   The discomfort continued. To this day, I do not fully understand the dynamics of what exactly happened around that table. It wasn't just Dona's, *'I wish he was mine'* vibe. It felt, to me, like *all* the woman had some type of agenda about Enes and the only other male at the table, his friend, Henry, also had some strange dynamic - could it possibly have been a table filled with jealousy and envy all round? They were already eating because, granted, we were very late. The only bit of comfort I had was my old friend, Annie. I had been confiding in her, on the phone, about Enes and she was the only person who I viewed as *neutral*. She was sitting opposite me. We ordered food and the food was incredibly disappointing, so much so that I felt like complaining but decided I wasn't hungry anyway and just left most of it. The conversation with the rest of the crowd was strained so I focused on Enes and Annie.

When the bill arrived it was passed around the table. I took out my card and had it ready to pay my portion. Enes took the bill and I asked him to let me know what I owed. He was sorting it out down on the one side of the table. There was a funny vibe around that too but I know from being in Turkey that they don't like dealing with cash directly out in the open and have little money boxes on the table at all the restaurants - but he's been living here a long time. Then Kendall noticed that I was still sitting with my card in front of me and said on the top of her voice,

*"Lesley hasn't paid yet"*. He then let me know how much I owed into the kitty. I had a feeling he was going to pay for me until that moment.

One of the women left soon after but before she did she came over and hugged Enes goodbye. I couldn't quite put my finger on it but was she hugging him a little bit too close like she was sending me a message? Enes then hopped chairs to go and sit opposite Henry. The whole night was just so uncomfortable. I think during that dinner, I realised that this had not been anything remotely comparable to a date - but now typing this out, I realise that we weren't really given a chance to feel relaxed and embraced at that dinner. There were so many underlying, other dynamics, going down. I went from feeling radiant to crumpled and energetically violated - and I lost my balance - I was literally just hanging in there, trying to put on a brave face. I couldn't wait to leave.

(Months later, Annie said I was like a lamb being led to slaughter – she had picked up the vibes and said the whole evening had been disgusting. Her words were, *"Where was the sisterhood?"* I had absolutely nobody in my corner that night, strangely enough including Annie – she said it had taken her so long to tell me this because she felt that I should have been more empowered).

Enes and I discussed the disjointed evening on our way home. At least we agreed on it. Both of us had picked stuff up but I don't think either of us had quite processed exactly what it was. All I knew was I just wanted to get in my car, as soon as possible, and run as fast as my little legs could carry me, away from him. I wanted him to love me - to want me and all I felt was - violated. I couldn't explain it.

When we got to his place, I asked him to grab my coat off the back seat, while I rummaged in my bag for my car keys. I headed straight to my car, which was parked just outside his front door. I hugged him goodbye. All he said was he liked my coat, as he passed it to me. I got in the car and squeezed his hand and all I could think of to say was, *"I'm sure we will chat about potatoes."* (This was in reference to the previous email he had sent me about potatoes being good for the skin so I should research it for my cream). Yes, I'm sure he would be happy to continue talking about potatoes every day for the next ten years, as long as I didn't ever mention that I was actually in love with him. I had had enough.

Driving home I understood why I had become so reclusive. If this was a taste of going out with my so-called friends then I didn't want any part of it and my friendship with Dona had long passed its sell by date – I was so over her too.

I got home - removed my clothes that I had lovingly dressed in for a potential date and got into bed. It would be hours of my mind churning, the events over and over, before I fell asleep. I just couldn't process any of it - what the hell was that all about? It came up for me that Enes should have paid for me. I had made him dinners at my house and had even sent him home with food for the next day. I never expected any man to pay for me but in this case, it was actually quite insulting that he didn't offer. Months of waiting to see what would happen, with Enes, were over. I felt so over it now...

## 18ᵗʰ May - Wednesday

Oh my gosh, I feel like I was splattered on a pavement by a steam roller. My bubble has finally burst and I'm oozing out, all messy and squishy, all over the place. The reality is too dreadful to face. I didn't want to let go of the dream of being with this man, I so admired - but I deserved so much more than this. I had taken this as far as I could possibly take it – there was nothing more I could do from my side. I had to let him go!

Later that day, I decided to cut him some slack and sent a message to say that even though the night had been weird and bizarre, it was still lovely to finally see his place. I thanked him for his open sharing and for the ride, with a smiley face. I was holding on to a very fine thread - my heart didn't want to let him go.

He replied that he was only just recovering from the work stress of the last few days and from the disjointed bunch of people from the night before.

I reacted - it felt like he was including me, along with the others. I had really had enough and I was now pushing the boundaries to breaking point.

Enes sent me an email saying that he did not include me in this scenario and that his two very dear friends, Henry and Sandy had also been there. He was just commenting about the group of people being disjointed. He also had noticed that Kendall had not even asked me how I am or didn't seem to appreciate the fact that I had made the effort. He was actually being nice but I think I was already on a real mission to push him away – a bit like when you know a relationship is over but you keep hanging in there, just in case you are wrong. And you hold on to a pin prick of hope that something may just, miraculously swoop in to rescue it from a horrible death - but there would be no heroes in this story.

He then went on to express that my question asking him if he was gay was inappropriate and that some straight men would have been very offended by it. He sounded extremely angry.

I replied, that the only reason I had for asking that question was because I was sexually attracted to him so it was actually a compliment. He said that I could just have been upfront about that and then he said that there would be no physical or emotional relationship between us - that he was just my time to time friend.

I guess this was the moment where I should have just cut the contact but a part of me found this really hard to actually believe – a guy writes to you virtually every day for months on end and when you have confessed your feelings he ends up making more contact than he did before. I had been so bewildered most of the time, I found it hard to even think clearly. So what exactly had he been doing having all that contact with me? I was painfully aware that we only got together from time to time but he had been energetically a part of my life for over five months. Why didn't he step out when I told him I had feelings for him – an emotionally intelligent man, who knew himself well enough to understand fully what 'emotionally unavailable' actually meant, would have known better. Had he been keeping a door open just in case he changed his mind? He never encouraged me to explore my options with the other guy - why? Surely if he hadn't felt anything for me, romantically, he would have encouraged me to go for it and find happiness with someone else? Perhaps, only now, he finally knew the answer to that question for sure and it was a definite, No — and from my side all I could do was find a way to cut it, as painful as it was going to be for me.

> *An emotionally avoidant man has been making choices, for a very long time, that support his own needs. He is doing what feels right for him. Nobody is to blame. We are all free to choose what we want for our lives and how we would like to conduct our relationships. Perhaps there was a small part of me that wanted to place some blame on his doorstep but the reality was, that I really could not find fault with Enes. He hadn't done anything wrong — all I could blame him for was that he didn't love me and he could not possibly be responsible for that. I only had once choice. I had to let him go and I had to find a way to reach closure and mend my broken heart. I had survived a life threatening illness as I'm sure other women have survived their own processes. I had been given survival resources that I could now draw upon. It was time to stand my ground in order to save myself one more time and heal.*

## 20<sup>th</sup> May - Thursday

My daughter called from the UK. She is one of the most well balanced women I have ever met. We had a long conversation and she gave me a completely different perspective on what had happened the night of the dinner party. She said he was trying to secure me - from talking about the night with the boys (he wanted me to know there were no women there), to telling me he is sexually *normal* to then letting me know that he had bumped into Dona. She said that he probably felt that paying for me was going to make a statement he wasn't ready to make.

If she was right then I had completely overreacted - I had *reacted* so badly to the whole situation but the bottom line was that he had stated loudly and clearly that there would *never* be anything romantic between us.

I made plans to go down to visit my close friend on the coast. I was feeling emotionally overwhelmed and had completely lost my centre. I felt that the best thing to do was remove myself from everything familiar to try and gain some perspective. I wrote a letter to Enes from my heart, expressing everything I really wanted to share with him - I didn't really care about the outcome anymore - well, that's what I told myself. The one thing I wasn't prepared to say was, *'I love you'* - I hinted at it - spoke about feelings but I did not say straight out, *"I love you"*.

My journal notebook was also nearly full and it was now time for a new one – and a new story. I would be starting a new phase in my life. I thought about all the journals I had in boxes - the orange covered one, the red one and a lot of black ones - each one of these journals could be given the name of some man who had been in my life at the time. Admittedly, there hadn't been one of these for years. I wrote in my journal, *'This journal will go into a box like all the others. It will mean nothing in a few years. This one will be The Enes Book.'* I started packing for Durban.

## 21ˢᵗ May - Friday

Enes sent me a message telling me how much he loved my long emails and said that he had never had such a deep sharing from a woman before. He went on to say that he was not part of this scenario and would not take anything on a personal level but would like to read it again and would like to comment on the patterns I keep reflecting out. He said it may be helpful for some other reason.

In that moment I felt extremely irate. I wasn't looking for a therapist – or to learn lessons, that he believed, he had been sent to teach me. The letter I had written him had been an authentic, incredible sharing from my heart - I had spent time and energy writing it from a balanced perspective - engaging with my goddess self who, I believed, also had some wisdoms to share. It was thought provoking and if anything, he could perhaps also have gained something from *really hearing me*. All I wanted was for him honour me as a woman - a woman who was now being punished for falling in love with him. There was no part of me, in that moment, that wanted to be seen as his wellness *subject* to be put under a microscope to scrutinise - supposedly to help me along on my journey, without him.

My reply message was quite patronising but I didn't care. I was hurting and needed to get on the road to Durban to begin figuring out how I was going to salvage my broken heart. I replied that what I had been attempting to express was that feelings are largely a mystery but he was welcome to do his *wellness passion* thing on it if he wanted to. I said I was leaving soon and had to run. I closed my journal and stuck it in a drawer.

From that moment onwards Enes mostly chose to ignore any messages I sent and I did try to send a few, including one that said maybe we could get together for a chat when I got back — it was going to be, face to face, as far as I was concerned, or nothing at all.

A couple days after I arrived in Durban he emailed me an Arnold Schwarzenegger poster with this quote: "*Your strength does not come from winning. Your struggles develop your strengths. When you go through hardship and decide not to surrender, that is strength.*"

I have no idea if there was a concealed message behind this. I had been trying to decipher too many hidden meanings behind all of the months of sharing, that perhaps never said exactly what they meant and I just couldn't even begin to piece together if this was a cryptic message or not - perhaps it just meant exactly what it said - absolutely nothing personal at all. It was time for my heart to say, 'Goodbye'.

*You may think that you are different from the other women he has met in his life and you may believe that you will be the one to help him through his issues and end up happily ever after with him. Think again. This man is intelligent enough to know where his boundaries are – he is not stupid. He knows he has issues. It's not up to you to want to fix him. If he ever decides he wants to make himself available for relationship, he will have to delve into his own issues, in his own time. It can only come from him and when and if this ever happens, you will never know unless he feels enough for you to make a decision that he wants to reach out and be with you for real. All you can do is live your own authentic life – don't wait – heal yourself and truly let him go.*

# How to Survive an Emotionally Unavailable Man

## What You Can and Can't Expect from an Emotionally Unavailable Man

Enes once said to me, in an email, that we must make the right type of investments in people. When we invest in an emotionally unavailable man, it is what investors would term 'high risk'. With a high risk investment your returns may be very high and exceed your expectations, if your predictions are accurate. The difference is that experienced investors take a calculated risk, believing that the odds are in their favour – they probably wouldn't touch this type of high risk investment because the odds of it paying out, according to their expectations, are very low but not impossible. It's a gamble and not a very calculated one. It's more like you are rolling dice and hoping that you will be the one in a million who wins big time. The question is, how much are you prepared to invest and what returns do you expect to get from your investment?

Do you have enough emotional resources in your piggy bank to deal with disappointment and a broken heart? Do you have enough back up savings in your self esteem account to never hear a sweet word from him about how much he cares about you? Do you have joint ventures with others who will support you when you realise that your risky investment is about to crash? Have you spent your money wisely on lots of home entertainment that you can escape into on cold and lonely nights? Do you have a charity you can tithe your surplus love to because you have so much of it to give and nobody around to give it to? Do you have some pets to cuddle while you wonder if your investment will turn around and hit an upward curve and surprise you with some real, meaningful returns – returns that would make all the waiting and wondering worthwhile? If you have all of these reserves to fall back on then perhaps you will survive and even flourish in your sort-of-ish-relationship with your emotionally unavailable man.

## The Women Who Fall for Emotionally Unavailable Men

The thought of a potential relationship with an emotionally unavailable man can initially be filled with excitement and there will be an air of anticipation around it. He is not an easy catch and because he is not falling at your feet, you believe that if you manage to reel this one in, it will show you just how valuable you are. This is largely sub-conscious and you will probably be unaware of how much of this anticipation is linked to the fact that you are purely looking to this man to validate you to prove you're worth it.

Woman who are more likely to stay glued and to persevere with this man are women with low self esteem who have a more insecure relationship style. The relationship with this man is characterised by a continual chase. This emotional chasing will result in a woman trying and trying, over and over again to break through his icy exterior. She is ultimately trying to prove her own self worth. A woman with high self esteem already knows she is worthy of love and will cut her losses and move on much quicker and more easily.

The positive side of this phenomenon is that a woman who is prepared to hang in there for an elusive, emotionally unavailable man shows character traits of tenacity, dedication and perseverance, over and above the call of duty. She is usually the type who will walk the extra mile for others and she is able to love more unconditionally than most. All of these are good qualities that if she directs appropriately, can lead to great achievements and fulfilling relationships. She just needs to focus her attention more inwardly to loving and accepting herself, as opposed to outwardly – wanting others to validate her.

These women can easily mistake this emotional chasing, as love. The more he pushes her away, the more she wants to be acknowledged by him, the more pain she feels, the more she imagines he will be the one to come around and soothe her. The original reasons why she liked him so much may become over shadowed by this habitual pattern of looking for ways to get his attention. If she was needy before she met him, her neediness now becomes exacerbated by his continual signs of rejection and the more needy she becomes, the more she wants him to be the one to make it all right by comforting her – she translates it into longing for him. It's a vicious circle that results in her experiencing the same pain over and over again. In reality she is doing it to herself and only she can break the pattern.

In the I-Ching (Ancient Chinese art of divination), it refers to a situation where somebody is seeking nurturing and instead they are given a stone. This is the perfect analogy for a woman who seeks the affections of an emotionally unavailable man. What she doesn't realise, is that the stone can also be a gift. You can't ask a stone to be anything other than what it is – it will not miraculously turn into a cuddly teddy bear. It has its own unique qualities. A stone may be a very cold, hard alternative to the warm intimacy you were seeking but it gives you an opportunity to turn inward to explore yourself in your own self-reflection. Embrace the gifts the stone offers you and see it for exactly what it is.

Invest in yourself and your own self-awareness and growth. Accept and love yourself exactly as you are now then realise that the only obstacle to becoming the positive, strong woman you aspire to be, is yourself.


## How Do I Deserve To Be Treated?


*"I deserve the best in all my relationships. I deserve people who show up in my life. I deserve and accept the best now."*

All the time that I was interacting with Enes, a part of me felt that I deserved more. I even wrote in my journal that I was looking for people who *showed up* in my life. If somebody isn't showing up for you, in a real way, there isn't very much you can do about it. It is their choice and you can't force them to fit into what you would like them to be. It is pointless blaming them – they may be doing the best they can with the resources available to them or they may just be oblivious to your needs and enjoying their own free time without you. Either way, this is the reality. If you can't change it, you just have to accept it. If you ascribe more to the relationship than there is in reality, you are merely hurting yourself. It's not their fault you want more and they can't or don't want to give you what your heart desires. You have two choices – you accept them exactly as they are (a part time person who is not showing up as you would like them to) or you can decide to walk away and take meaningful steps to begin attracting people into your life who are able to and want to meet your needs.

I love this affirmation by Louise Hay, in her book, You Can Heal Your Life - *"I forgive.....................(person's name) for not being what I wanted him to be for me. I forgive him and set him free. I am free and he is free"*.

## Sex and the Emotionally Avoidant Man

Emotionally unavailable men are disassociated from their emotions. This may have taken them time and practise to get right. Once they have achieved the goal of removing themselves from the anxiety, or potential pain, attached to intimacy and sex, they are less likely to become sexually involved with somebody they genuinely care about or could potentially end up getting close to. The emotionally unavailable man may have experienced a lot of pain or many disappointments, in their past and they view getting too close as the culprit that had caused them these uncomfortable negative emotions. They have taught themselves to avoid real connection. Anything that may challenge their comfort zone, of being disassociated, is a threat to the status quo they have achieved.

I will never presume to know much about what men, as a whole, think sexually. Without a penis of my own, to think for me, I don't have direct experiential knowledge in this area. I have, however, researched the emotionally unavailable man's sexuality. One emotionally avoidant man stated that just because he is emotionally unavailable, does not mean that he is dead. He still finds women attractive and will sleep with an attractive woman if she'll let him. There are varying sides of the spectrum but many emotionally avoidant men would rather sleep with women they can objectify than a woman who may get emotionally attached. Their sexual preferences can range from prostitutes to strip clubs to casual sex with strangers, porn or to no sex at all.

I never really knew whether Enes was sexually active but he did insinuate that just because he didn't chase after women, didn't mean he wasn't sexual and he said that sex was different from a relationship. He may or may not have been hiring call girls to satisfy his sexual needs. I suspected he did but I was only guessing and may be completely wrong. Personally I didn't have too much of an issue with this. It is less destructive than an emotionally unavailable man sleeping with women that could become emotionally attached and then turning around afterwards and saying it was their fault – they knew from the outset what they were getting into. If an emotionally avoidant man sleeps with women for a money exchange, it is a mutually beneficial transaction between two consenting adults and the boundaries are clear. I do not advocate this type of sex because I have some issues around it energetically, but that is another topic altogether.

If you have opened this door for an emotionally unavailable man, knowing he was unavailable for a deeper relationship, and he stepped in, then in reality, you have to take responsibility. You allowed somebody, you have feelings for, to treat you casually. Decide what it is that you really want and don't doubt yourself or compromise that. You may end up feeling degraded, hurt, angry and violated. You cannot blame him if he was upfront and warned you.

Be gentle on yourself and put it down to experience. Learn from it and work on moving on. Sex is often thought of as a gateway to relationships. A relationship requires more substance on many different levels. An emotionally avoidant man can conveniently remove his emotions from pretty much any situation so why should sex be any different – he is not going to suddenly become emotionally available after a great shag, no matter how good it was.

Also don't assume that just because an emotionally unavailable man prefers to go home to his own bed that he is sleeping with someone else. It may just be because he prefers his own sanctuary - the space and privacy to sleep alone.

## Can an Emotionally Unavailable Man Be a Nice Guy?

Just because a man is emotionally unavailable, doesn't mean he isn't a nice guy with sensitivity, high standards and good values. From the outside looking in, he can appear to be a great catch and have all the ingredients women are looking for in a man. Enes was a genuinely nice guy. He was kind, caring and decent. That in itself, didn't give me the go ahead to fall for him hook, line and sinker. He had all the criteria I wanted in a man except for that one big issue – he wasn't available for a relationship. It was me that invested in him inappropriately. He was unable to give me what I wanted.  He could have been an amazing lifelong friend. He was wise, switched on and very supportive in everything else, except where it came to anything on a personal level that involved him in any way. And I wanted personal.

An emotionally unavailable man doesn't have to be the bad guy your mother warned you about. He is perfectly entitled not to want emotional or physical bonds that tie him down. There is nothing wrong with him deciding on what type of lifestyle suites him best. It's up to you to decide if his lifestyle choices are right for you. That is really the bottom line. The decision is entirely yours to make and nobody is to blame.

## Can You Just Be His Friend?

My wise woman thought I could evolve beyond my feelings for him and overcome what my heart was longing for in him. Perhaps you can find a way to do this. I couldn't. I had fallen too deeply for him – my heart wanted what my heart wanted and no amount of Zen Philosophy about it was going to change that. It's incredibly sad to lose somebody altogether because of this - in my situation, getting out was the only rational choice for me.

When investors realise that they have made a bad investment and are losing money and there are no signs of improvement, they often take their money out and 'park it' in a money market account until they can decide where to next. It's a safe place to keep it and to consolidate. It's a cooling off period – taking time out – giving it breathing space. Looking back, in hindsight, I would have to say that this is perhaps my biggest regret. I was too quick to 'react' to my own feelings of disappointment. I could have spent more time, allowing myself to stand back and apart from it.

Many philosophies speak about becoming the observer, being able to watch events, in your life, from a type of distance. I understand that when it comes to love, it seems to be a type of overwhelming craziness, with a mind of its own and can be all consuming – songs have been sung about this – without love and heartbreak the music industry would go bankrupt. So without negating your feelings, try to become the watcher - listen carefully to your own self and also listen carefully to what the other person is saying to you or even what they are not saying (in this case be careful not to make assumptions or reading too much into it and creating your own story around it but the unspoken can give you some clues or hints). As previously pointed out, this man is unlikely to use sweet words or ascribe a label to the relationship (he would probably prefer the words association or friendship). It is likely you have already been doing a lot of trying to read between the lines to make sense of it all. Strive now to listen with an open mind and then take what happens purely at face value.

If your emotionally unavailable man is the nice guy you think he is, he will not go out of his way to lie to you or to make false promises. It's up to you to really 'hear him'. If you do find out that he is lying to you then he is definitely not worth a moment more of your investment. That will be your queue to just walk away. If you do believe that he is in integrity then there is no harm creating a bit of distance and spaces between your contact, for you to find your balance and decide if you want to go forward, knowing what you now know. Are you prepared to just be his friend and will this ultimately be good for you? Answer this question honestly and you will know what to do.


## Positive Steps to Recreate Your Social Life


You probably won't feel like even thinking about other men because you are attached to the idea of your amazing emotionally unavailable man - nobody out there will be able to match up to him. Nobody can compare to the one that got away, right. I suggest that you consider meeting new men as friends. There are lots of lonely men out there who are also looking for woman to go out with or just spend time with.

Dating sites are not only for finding romantic relationships. You can say, on your profile, you are looking to meet men as friends to socialise with (this is what I did when I was in the UK and I met a couple of men I could have friendships with). Even if you don't feel like it, give it a try. Meet some men for coffee and see if you can find a friend or two. If you need some healing time first, that's also okay but don't sit around for too long, nursing your broken heart. Start engaging life again. If you already have a good social life and still feel the pain of your unrequited love then just give it time. That's all you can do.

The most important thing you do, is to realise that you have to invest correctly in this emotionally avoidant man before you create more pain and heartache for yourself – not giving or expecting more than he can give or deciding not to invest in him anymore at all. I knew for sure that I couldn't just be Enes's friend. I felt it would be dishonest to pretend that I could. I needed to be authentic about how I felt. When I realised that he didn't feel the same, the only sane choice for me was to remove myself, as hard as that was for me - and still is sometimes. I would love to have him really show up in my life but it's just a dream. I doubt it will ever happen.

# Can an Emotionally Unavailable Man Fall in Love with You

I believe that love is the ultimate healer of all dysfunctions in the world. Everybody has been gifted with the capacity to love. Nobody is born emotionally unavailable. Your emotionally avoidant man will find it difficult to identify his own feelings – he may feel disturbed by his attraction to you. It could bring up gut level fear but he may not acknowledge this or even admit this to himself. The very last item on his list of avenues to explore, to identify exactly what it is he is feeling, is love. He may never get to this as he explains it all away with more rational explanations. There was a song by the band, 10CC, in the eighties, I'm Not In Love. The song says he's not in love and she mustn't forget that. He says that it's just a silly phase he's going through. He explains that he likes to see her but then goes on to say that it doesn't really mean much to him. He keeps a picture of her on his wall but it's purely to hide a stain. He likes to call her but she mustn't make a fuss about it or tell her friends about the two of them. He tells her he's not in love - just because. At the end of the song he repeats, over and over, that big boys don't cry.*

This man is clearly smitten and in love with her. It is a case of, *'the guy he doth protest too much'*. The songwriter has a degree of emotional intelligence because he ultimately understands the reason why he just can't go there. He was told over and over that boys don't cry and he learned to suppress and hide his feelings so as not to show weakness. He is still carrying issues from his childhood that messed him up – he knows this and admits it. (It is not a given that an emotionally unavailable man's issues come from childhood. Their issues can stem from other pain so don't assume to know what the underlying cause is - it can be related to a number of traumas or emotionally taxing events. You will only understand the reasons if he shares it with you and it's doubtful he will.)

If - and it's a big if - your emotionally avoidant man has fallen in love with you, he will first have to come to that realisation on his own. Then if he decides that he values you more than he wants to hold on to his issues, he will have to come to a decision, of his own accord, that he needs to work through and overcome his issues. All of the above, do not involve you in any way whatsoever. You are not his therapist and you are not there to *fix him*. Good luck to you if you think you can try. He will probably not take very kindly to it and may just push you even further away.

An emotionally unavailable man will respect you more if he sees that you value yourself and that you are not prepared to be a doormat for him to wipe his dirty feet on. The most pro-active stance that you can take is to know yourself and work on the part that you played within this - dare I call it - relationship. Be the best person you can be. Concentrate on your own growth and development and be authentic to your own needs and wants. You are entitled to ask for what you want and you are entitled to want whatever it is that you want. Be prepared for the reality that it may not be with this emotionally avoidant man. He is probably too busy roaming around the vast expanses of places to go or people he could meet in the future or simply enjoying his own alone time – basking in his own independence and freedom.

Whether you think you have won this battle or lost, love actually always wins in the end. Just think about it this way – nobody can tell you who you can or cannot love. Your love is not dependent on outer circumstances or whether or not it is returned to you. There is a freedom in knowing that you are free to love whoever you choose. You don't have to stop the flow of love, just the expectation and longing that love has created in you. Let the story go and live your own, authentic life in love.

* I would love to include the lyrics to this song because it encapsulates the emotionally unavailable man so well but due to copyright laws and the publishing company not replying to my email request, I am unable to. I suggest you listen to the words of this song online.
Songwriters: Eric Stewart / Graham Gouldman
I'm Not in Love lyrics © Sony/ATV Music Publishing LLC, Schubert Music Publishing Inc.

# Afterword - Two Years Later

I did try a few times to salvage the connection with Enes because I still believed we had met for a reason - and that reason had not been fully realised but I was largely doing it alone. He backed off, at first fairly gently and then to a point of ghosting me. It became quite degrading and I felt like those women who simply can't take a hint from men - I never wanted to be labelled a *stalker*. I even decided to delete his phone number off my phone for a while but when I went to delete it, the numerology in the numbers was astounding – I had never really studied the number before. The first three digits were a major service provider then it was my birthday separated by a seven (a spiritual number) then my son's birthday numbers then my daughter's birthday. I was never going to forget his phone number, even if I wanted to but I deleted it anyway. What was the point of having a contact who didn't want to have any contact?

My wild, feral cat had left for good. I held on to the belief that he must have felt something for me - who messages and emails a woman, for five months - virtually every day for three, with no interest in her whatsoever, which was what he was now trying to tell me - he felt no connection to me. It was a bitter pill to swallow and was painful for my damaged ego to hear. I didn't realise, at the time that I was not going to get over him very easily and that distance in days, months and now years, would not fully heal the wound.

I fell in love with an emotionally unavailable man. For a long time, I thought about him, at least once every day. I went to Namibia and painted sand dunes, I moved house into a lovely furnished apartment, in what used to be a healing centre and then I decided to pack up and visit my daughter in the UK for six months. Every so often, during all these life changes, I messaged Enes just to check in with him and he always replied - he had obviously gotten over ghosting me (After some distance and space I had put his number back into my phone).

I did a lot of work on myself and a lot of healing. I shared some articles I wrote with him and he seemed open to hearing me on that level. I did work on forgiveness for my past and I shared some of this work with him. He told me that I was vibrating on a different level to the mainstream and I must stop expecting people to understand me because they can't, even if they try. This was a huge compliment and showed that he respected and admired me. He said I must believe in myself and continue doing what I do best - writing, being emotional, being creative - he said I must not doubt myself.

We got close to seeing one another again. He even promised to bring some *'Turkish Flavour'* into my life, which was *the* most *flirty* thing I had ever heard him say but then he said he would make a plan to meet me for coffee, closer to the end of the month when work wasn't so busy. The end of the month was weeks away and I got the feeling that I would just be going back on to a round-a-bout with him. I knew that I wouldn't be able to handle that all over again. I messaged him something about how I always undersold myself with men - it was general and not accusing him of anything and he emailed me a letter saying that I had always made things bigger than they were. I told him, that if seeing him again was completely dependent on how I behave or don't behave, then it wasn't going to work - and that just gave him an excuse to back off again completely.

I am still not completely over him but I have healed myself emotionally. I sometimes question whether I will spend the rest of my life loving this elusive, man and stop wondering if one day he may just pop his head through the cat flap and come and curl up on my lap. I understand, intellectually that all of this could have been an illusion of my own creation and could still, very well be but my intuitive woman knows deep down that I have a love for him - it's not so painful anymore and I have moved on but every now and then, it still overwhelms me.

What could I have done differently – oh, there is so much I would do differently, knowing what I now know and while typing up this journal, I realised that hindsight is a real *bitch*. The insights I have incorporated into my journal have been part of my healing. I hope that others, in my situation, can use my open and honest account of this experience as an opportunity for them to self-reflect. Every human interaction is unique - not all emotionally unavailable men are the same but many of the traits follow these same patterns of behaviour.

I now repeat something my father once said to me, *"You don't only have to learn from your own mistakes - you can learn from other people's mistakes before you even have to make your own'*. You can use my experience to transform your own life path into a much more life affirming process. So what would you have done differently if you were in my shoes? Follow your answers, follow your own intuitions and see if you can find a different ending...

May your light always shine brightly.

Lilith White

# SIMPATICO

I heard some lines from a poem, a few years ago, quoted by Sean Penn in the Movie 21 Grams. Something in these few simple lines resonated deeply with me. This poem, I wrote for Enes, a couple years after our meeting, matches what the poet was expressing about synchronistic, profoundly *meant to be* meetings. I begin my own poem with a quote of the first few lines of the poem, The Earth Turned to Bring Us Closer by Venezuelan poet, Eugenio Montejo, translated by Peter Boyle.


"The earth turned to bring us closer
It spun on itself and within us
And finally joined us together in this dream"

The same year a husband dies
A man is boarding a plane
Both him and the widow
Spinning in time
Towards a destiny unknown
Within them a new life germinates

And it spins for decades more
From parallels to paradoxes
Through relationships of pain
In which they are carved
Into opposites…both deepen
One in thought, one in heart

The clock ticked as if
Its infinite hands meant something
Stopping not for a moment
Not even a second
At the time they were brought together
In this lifetime, to meet

All the places, all the faces had been lining them up
The moments of not meeting
And not meeting again
Moving inside of them
Until finally they were aligned
To come together in this dream

In a mirage or perhaps a reality
Orchestrated on another level
She sensed the turning within
A compulsion to follow the direction of the movement
And she knew that this was more than chance
As if it ever was or could have been…

She was too far removed from the chit chat of life
Not to have resonated with kindred soul
A mirror of her own mind
And if it wasn't so…surely it would have just passed her by
Like the flutter of a breeze
Or the bending of the blades of grass
Where he had sat

How could he not have felt the turning
…the eclipses, the ever waxing and waning
That had brought them to that place of simpatico
He said she had made it bigger than it really was
She thought perhaps he was right
It is not usual to deem such every day events as remarkable…

Millenniums had passed between them
And many lives through them
Millions had met, never to meet again
Countless had loved another without return
People had left for one destination and arrived in another
Yet absence had brought her nearer, not further away

Nothing that was ever possible becomes impossible
Is love made manifest purely by two co-creators having the same dream
Or perhaps it was he who had diminished the miraculous
As if he ever could have…
If he was even real or ever could have been…

<u>Other Titles by This Author</u>

The Other Side of My Reflection by Lilith White – A woman possessed by more than a desire to find her soul mate.

Available on Amazon Books, Kindle and Kobo.

<u>https://www.amazon.com/Other-Side-my-Reflection-Lilith-White/s?k=The+Other+Side+of+my+Reflection+by+Lilith+White&rh=n%3A283155</u>

<u>https://www.kobo.com/ww/en/ebook/the-other-side-of-my-reflection</u>

Please note: I am not a qualified therapist and the insights in this book have been gained through my own personal experience and through reading extensively about the topic. There are wonderful life coaches and therapists who have experience in helping people overcome emotional difficulties. If you need help do not hesitate to find a therapist or coach who suits your needs. There is no harm in reaching out for help.